FEARFUL RAVAGES:
YELLOW FEVER IN NEW ORLEANS,
1796-1905

This book is dedicated to my guides to New Orleans

Dr. Karen M. La Paro

and

Dr. John R. Peacock, III

Louisiana Life Series, No. 15

FEARFUL RAVAGES:
YELLOW FEVER IN NEW ORLEANS,
1796-1905

BENJAMIN H. TRASK

Center for Louisiana Studies
University of Louisiana at Lafayette
2005

Center for Louisiana Studies
University of Louisiana at Lafayette
P.O. Box 40831
Lafayette, LA 70504-0831

ISBN: 1-887366-64-4
Library of Congress Control Number: 2005907870

Printed on acid-free paper.

http://cls.louisiana.edu

CONTENTS

ACKNOWLEDGMENTS

In completing the research for this little volume, I traveled to libraries and archives from New York to New Orleans. When not able to make the trip, I was fortunate to gain material through interlibrary loans and written correspondence.

As I researched, dozens of public services personnel helped me in my quest. Wallace Dailey of the Roosevelt Collection of the Houghton Library of Harvard University provided me with information concerning the Pres. Theodore Roosevelt and his trip to New Orleans. The staff of the Williams Research Center of The Historic New Orleans Collection, Katherine Fuller McKenzie, Reference Librarian at the College of William and Mary, the reference librarians and archives staff at the University of Virginia, and the South Carolina Historical Society in Charleston were equally as helpful. In Washington, the staffs at the Library of Congress rare book collection and manuscripts division and National Archives and Records Administration provided prompt assistance to me among an ocean of researchers. Much research was completed at university medical libraries. The reference staffs at the Medical College of Virginia in Richmond, the health science libraries at the University of Virginia, University of North Carolina at Chapel Hill, and the New York Academy of Medicine in New York City all helped with up-to-date reference material and directed me to nineteenth-century journals.

A trio of ladies that always help with my projects are my mother-in-law, Margaret N. La Paro, my wife, Susan L. Trask, and my sister-in-law, Dr. Karen M. La Paro. Karen allowed me to stay at her home while researching at the University of Virginia and provided me with information concerning West Nile virus. Peggy sent articles to me on mosquitoes and diseases found in the daily presses. And Sue, who has read enough about yellow fever to lecture on the disease, located articles, proofread, and gave me both time and encouragement to finish the manuscript.

A fellow student of yellow fever, James K. Rindfleisch, biologist for York County Mosquito Control and former president of the Virginia

Mosquito Control Association, read and offered comments and encouragement. Colleague and fellow Hokie Leslie Brooks edited much of the epilogue and personal note. Two fine gentlemen answered my questions concerning the characteristics and impact of certain chemical agents used as disinfects and fumigants. They are Col. David W. Dick, a former United States Army chemical warfare officer and biology teacher, and Dr. Clinton W. Stallard, formerly medical director of the Newport News Shipyard and a corporate medical director for British Petroleum in the United States.

Help with images and information was provided by Catherine C. Kahn, archivist of the Touro Infirmary in New Orleans, and my friends at the Mariners' Museum also provided images and support.

A cemetery scene during an 1870s epidemic.

INTRODUCTION

If Thou Delay, how many lives are lost!
We ask a blessing never prized till now—
*The white gift of Thy frost!**

New Orleans is one of the premier vacation destinations in the United States. Just a walk through the French Quarter can make the trip worthwhile. For those who cannot make the journey, the flavor and sounds of Louisiana travel well. The ambiance of the Big Easy has become so dominant that multi-cultural food and music festivals inspired by the people of the Pelican State thrive across the United States. Even Mardi Gras has scores of imitators.

Unfortunately, not all impressions of the Crescent City have been so inviting. In the nineteenth century, New Orleans was stigmatized by an extremely high mortality rate. One of the major causes of this frightening annual death toll was yellow fever. The sporadic arrival of fever caused tens of thousands of citizens to flee; while at the same time, anxious neighbors in nearby towns tracked the fever's movement. The severity of yellow fever epidemics was erratic and puzzled physicians. In some years, thousands of people perished; at other times, only a handful died. This ghastly phenomenon appeared in the summer and remained until late autumn and marked New Orleans as a dangerous place. For decades the layman in New Orleans determined the first frost was the sign that the fever was quickly fading, and for that reason residents hoped and prayed for this meteorological blessing.

Despite the boastful claims by various healers, yellow fever's true cause eluded doctors for centuries. Sages assumed the fever's presence in North American seaports was one of the telltale signs of the evils of urban living. Filth, vermin, stifling heat, free-roaming livestock, and crowded living conditions characterized many port towns. Physicians believed that fever poisons, transported by miasmic gases, rose from amongst all this wretchedness. Other theories also abounded. Mariners

* A stanza from "Waiting For The Frost," *Harper's Weekly* 22 (October 19, 1878): 837.

1

sailing in the Caribbean waters especially feared the disease. The virus devastated crews and entire regiments. British and French surgeons penned hundreds of letters, treatises, and books on the yellow fever's causes, cures, symptoms, and prevention. In reality, few of these writings aided in the eradication of the fever, and many of these false cures did more harm than good to the suffering patients.

In 1647, New England may have suffered the first outbreak of the disease in the British coastal Atlantic colonies, or it may have appeared first in the 1660s in present-day New York City. Regardless of the original outbreak, following the emergence of thirteen colonies as the United States, yellow fever regularly appeared in New York, Philadelphia, Norfolk, Charleston, and Baltimore. Fevers dictated life cycles in the cities. Those urbanites who could afford to leave vacationed at mountain springs during the warm "sickly" season. Planters resided in their townhouses only in the cooler months. During the 1790s, federal representatives in Philadelphia recessed their legislative sessions during the hot summer months to avoid the sticky weather. At the same time, the character of local politicians and clergy members were measured by their willingness to remain with the fever sufferers during an epidemic.

Until the 1820s, the northern and mid-Atlantic seaboard cities of New York, Philadelphia, and Baltimore suffered the harshest epidemics. After this decade there were no major epidemics in the Northeast. It did, however, continue to terrorize the South. By the 1850s, Americans perceived the fever strictly as a Southern plague as it erupted irregularly from Norfolk to Galveston. New Orleans held the dubious honor as the hub of this deadly activity. Religious and civic leaders expanded or established cemeteries to accommodate the remains of thousands of yellow fever victims. At least as early as the 1790s and until 1905 yellow fever periodically ravaged the people of New Orleans. For various reasons, more people died of yellow fever in New Orleans than in any other city in the county.

So prevalent was yellow fever in the warmer latitudes of the Western Hemisphere that it was known by more than 150 different names. Northern European victims of the fever exhibited jaundiced-looking complexions. For this reason the disease was dubbed yellow fever, Bronze

John, or the saffron scourge. Among Spanish-speaking peoples the illness was known as *vomito negro*, or the black vomit, because the sick regurgitated partially digested blood, often with a coffee ground-like color and consistency. Many immigrants and travelers fell to the fever. Thus, natives called the disease the strangers' fever or strangers' disease. Sailors knew it as yellow jack because laws required shipmasters to fly a yellow flag, or jack, when their ships came into port with fever-stricken passengers or crew members.

Despite its reputation for epidemics, New Orleans was one of the key metropolitan centers of the young nation, in part because of its prime location about 110 miles north of the Mississippi delta on the eastern bank of the great river. In 1860, it was the country's fourth largest city and by far the greatest in the South. It was also a diverse city, attracting a variety of fortune seekers and immigrant nationalities. African American and Irish stevedores unloaded millions of bales of raw cotton from river steamboats onto ocean-going ships to be transported to the textile mills of Europe and New England. As draymen worked the waterfront, immigrants from Germany and Ireland disembarked. These newcomers provided the labor needed to dig canals and handle cargo. As a commercial center, employees of the customhouse tracked the movement of cotton. Taxing exported cotton was a major source of revenue for the United States. In addition to cotton, sugar and a portion of the harvested bounty of the Midwest filled the port while awaiting shipment to world markets.

In the 1800s, the people of New Orleans experienced tremendous commercial growth, wars, demographic changes, Reconstruction, depression, and corruption. Through all these happenings, the threat of yellow fever influenced how decisions were made. The scope of this brief study provides an overview of the epidemics in New Orleans from 1796 until 1905 within their social, ethnic, medical, military, and economic contexts. In conjunction with this overview, the city's leadership role in the modern public health movement and a retelling of how the humanitarians of Louisiana applied their fever expertise to relieve stricken citizens of other states are also explored.

Frost was a powerful meteorological portent that signaled the close of a yellow fever epidemic. In this engraving from *Harper's Weekley* (October 19, 1878) titled "Plague-stricken—waiting for the frost," a woman in black, stricken with fever, is drawing comfort from her companion in white, who peers into the future searching for a hard frost. Image courtesy of the Mariners' Museum Library and Archives, Newport News, VA.

Chapter One

ESTABLISHING TRADE AND A REPUTATION, 1790s-1820s

All strangers shun New Orleans from June to November to escape the deadly yellow fever. I arrived just at the end of such a terrible, all-ravaging epidemic. *

Trade drove life in early New Orleans. The lure of money attracted people as strongly as any gold rush. Even those individuals who arrived against their will, such as enslaved Africans and exiles, only enriched the global blend of humanity and greatly contributed to the effort to generate commerce. Samuel Cumings, an experienced riverboat man, concluded "probably no other city in the world contains a greater variety of population of black and white, than New Orleans. Inhabitants from every state in the Union, and from every country in Europe, mixed with Creoles, and all shades of the colored population, form an astonishing contrast of manner, language, and complexion."[1]

Intertwined with the pursuit of wealth in New Orleans, yellow fever lurked. For more than a hundred years, the fever was one of the most dreaded epidemical diseases in North America. It terrorized mariners as well as coastal residents in river towns and seaports. This fear sparked interest in health reform, public sanitation, and federal quarantine regulations, and marked New Orleans as a fever-ridden pesthole.[2]

The deadly pathogen that causes yellow fever is an arbovirus (arthropod-borne). In the United States, the *Aëdes (Stegomyia) aegypti* mosquito was the carrier, or vector, of the disease. (As of printing, the name for this mosquito has undergone debate. The subgenus *Stegomyia* was elevated to generic status in 2005, rendering the new name *Stegomyia aegypti*. Yet, many scientists are reluctant to rename this notorious mosquito in order to avoid confusion and misidentification. As such, the mosquito will be indentified throughout this book by its historical

* Savoie Lottinville, ed., *Paul Wilhelm, Duke of Württemberg: Travels in North America, 1822-1824* (Norman, OK, 1973), 34.

name, *Aëdes aegypti.*) Remarkably, this insect thrives best in an urban environment. The female of the species needs the protein found in human blood to ovulate. She infects individuals with the virus after acquiring the disease from an infectious human. There is only about a three-day window of time in which the insect can contract the virus from an infected human. After the virus has spread and incubated in the mosquito for a couple of days to a few weeks, the mosquito can infect other humans for the rest of the insect's short life. Studies have shown the virus can "winter over" or be transferred to the eggs of a vector mosquito. This feature, however, is not thought to be a factor of the North American epidemics. Consequently, the virus had to be reintroduced from warmer lands, where the virus was endemic.[3]

As a city-dwelling, "domesticated," day-feeding creature, the *A. aegypti* normally lives her life within a few hundred yards from where she was born. She is not a strong flyer. Nonetheless, in the 1800s, the insect gained great mobility when it traveled on ships, trains, and riverboats. The *A. aegypti* detects humans by the emission of carbon dioxide, amino acids, heat, and other cues. Able to consume more than her own weight in blood, after feeding, the female seeks relatively clean, calm water in hard surface containers to lay her eggs. She may lay her eggs in more than one location. This habit of not putting all of her "eggs in one basket," helps to insures the survival of at least some of her offspring. Newborn mosquito larvae, or wrigglers, consume decayed matter and microorganisms. In about ten days, they emerge from the water and take flight.[4]

Most scientists claim that slave traders imported the disease to the Americas from West Africa. Scientists point to a pair of factors that support this view. African slaves demonstrated a resistance to the fever. From these observations, many nineteenth-century physicians incorrectly concluded that slaves were immune to the fever. Also, modern specialists note African primates are less susceptible to the virus than their American "cousins." The monkeys in South America and Africa remain a reservoir for the virus and this phenomenon is one of the reasons the virus may never be eradicated. As long as there are wild primates, there will be a reserve for the fever pathogen.

In New Orleans, thousands of rainwater cisterns, gutters, troughs, barrels, and buckets made excellent incubators for the insect. This ar-

hailing from New Orleans being quarantined in foreign ports. Doctors and the general populace promoted a plethora of cures. He noted the ship that was singled out as the purveyor of the fever lost almost the whole crew. Pontalba differed with local physicians concerning the exact nature of fever. He reported to his wife "Our physicians are of the opinion that it is the yellow fever of Philadelphia. The same symptoms, they say, characterize it, but I am not in accord with their opinion."[10]

Yellow jack returned in 1799, and the reaction by the public to pestilence was much like the previous epidemic. The following year, Atty. Gen. Pedro Dulcidio Barran expressed his concerns for the future of the city in a letter to the municipal government. His remarks, like those of Pontalba, heralded discussions on sanitation, drainage, quarantine, and the origins of the fever. Dulcidio criticized his neighbors for their slovenly habits. He suggested planting trees to prevent the sun from heating pools of freestanding water, which emit harmful vapors. Coffins needed to be laced with lime that encouraged rapid decomposition of the remains. Finally, Dulcidio proposed that incoming ships and their cargoes needed health inspections. A contemporary of Dulcidio, merchant and naturalized American James Pitot, declared "No, Lower Louisiana is not an unhealthy place. Only in its city is centered the pollution that tears it down. An active government, benevolent and enlightened, would have soon eliminated it."[11]

Beginning in 1800, France began to exhibit an interest in re-establishing itself in the Western Hemisphere. In October 1800 France reacquired Louisiana via the secret Treaty of San Ildefonso; however, French officials would not exercise their control over the territory until late in 1803. In the meantime French ruler Napoleon Bonaparte dispatched troops to regain the island of Saint-Domingue (Haiti). Faced with former slaves under inspired leadership and debilitated by yellow jack, thousands of French soldiers perished. Among the French fever victims was Gen. Charles Victor Emmanuel Leclerc. The rebellion and fever consumed the lives of 60,000 French soldiers. His troops driven off the island, Napoleon then cut his losses and sold the vast Louisiana territory to the United States.[12]

The turbulent experiences of the first United States governor, William Charles Coles Claiborne, were tragically representative of the

9

American officials trying to assert control over the city in the face of friction among competing nationalities and seasonal pestilence. When the governor and his wife, Elizabeth (Elizah) W. Lewis Claiborne, contracted the fever in 1804, Joseph Briggs, the governor's private secretary, maintained correspondence with Sec. of State James Madison. In reporting on the health of the couple, Briggs informed Madison "that altho a convalescent so delicate in his [the governor's] Health and so unfavorable [is] the Season[,] the probability of a relapse is by no means removed." Elizah Claiborne appeared to be recovering, but her illness returned, in Briggs's words, with "such alarming Symptoms that almost every hope of preserving her life is extinguished." The governor survived. Elizah died apparently the same day as the couple's daughter, Cornelia. The governor also lost his brother-in-law. The fever also claimed Briggs, and H. Brown Trist, the collector of customs. That year the fever proved "particularly fatal to Strangers." In 1809, Claiborne's second wife, Clarissa Duralde, also fell to the fever.[13]

Monuments to William C.C. Claiborne's wives in St. Louis Cemetery #1, New Orleans; Elizah, at left, and Clarissa, at right, both yellow fever casualties.

In 1796, James Pitot was one of the many international residents of New Orleans. He was born in France and moved to the French West Indies. Following a slave revolt, he fled to his homeland. He then came to the United States, became a naturalized citizen, and resided in Philadelphia before settling in New Orleans. Pitot, a successful merchant, became the mayor and later a judge. He was a man of vision and assumed that New Orleans could become "one of the richest markets in the New World." Moreover, he was frustrated by the failure of the Spanish and French governments to maximize the business opportunities afforded by the gulf port, and perturbed that the local authorities failed to enforce sanitary regulations that he felt would free the town of fever. Pitot acknowledged, however, that the Americans foresaw the potential for New Orleans. With the United States' acquisition of the Louisiana Purchase and invention of the cotton gin, the hope the Americans prophesied came to fruition. River boatmen transported grain and the bounty of America's heartland down the Mississippi. Sugar and cotton plantations in the region mushroomed and the Crescent City funneled the fiber to the spinning textile mills of New England and Western Europe.[14]

Not long after Pitot's observations, Americans arrived in large numbers, and the river town began to grow. The population grew from 17,240 in 1810 to well over 150,000 inhabitants fifty years later. With this growth developed a deadly pattern of high mortality among the endless stream of new arrivals. In the early 1800s, Judge Richard Claiborne of New Orleans cleverly framed the reason that so many entrepreneurs ventured to the port in the antebellum years. He wrote to a colleague "New Orleans may be compared to a Plate of Honey. Thousands of insects come & satiate themselves with the sweet food, and die—but where one dies, a thousand visit the delicious repast. So it is with men—where their interests lie, they'll come to the place, tho' death stare them in the face."[15]

Some of those who came were part of the construction workforce. In the midst of an epidemic, architect and urban planner Benjamin Henry Latrobe complained that the pestilence "[had] consumed or driven away the majority of those whom experience has proved to be most subject to it, the young strangers." In 1819, Latrobe fretted over his waterworks project, relaying "The epidemic now prevailing, and the fear of it, have dispersed almost all my workmen." Likewise, a federal government survey report claimed "The prevalence

Latrobe's New Orleans Waterworks

11

of sickness in Louisiana during the past season has materially interfered with field operations in that State."[16]

Yellow fever also often extracted a fatal toll on the entrepreneurs and workers associated with commerce such as stevedores, draymen, warehousemen, stonemasons, keelboat men, and canal diggers. Yellow jack's reputation influenced settlement patterns, and suppressed, delayed, and caused the rerouting of shipments. Competing towns magnified New Orleans' association with the fever in an effort to draw business away from the Crescent City. Louisiana politicians, newspaper editors, merchants, and some physicians collectively countered these claims by suppressing information related to outbreaks. As rumor of the fever's approach increased, mistrust grew, leading surrounding communities to block communications and commercial and humanitarian interaction ceased. Throughout the nineteenth century, the disease was as much a part of doing business in New Orleans as the rise and fall of the Mississippi River.[17]

The fever's reputation also concerned American military and naval personnel who worked to control the new territorial acquisition. The U.S. Navy stationed warships and garrisoned Marines in Louisiana. The Marines were billeted in the city and at nearby Camp Claiborne. In 1805, the Marine contingent even departed because of the unhealthy environment and returned in the fall. In the summer of 1809, naval personnel suffered from an unidentified outbreak thought to have been yellow fever.[18]

With the fever raging, in 1811, Claiborne sailed to Baton Rouge to suppress a slave rebellion. Fearful of yellow jack, the governor intervened on behalf of two Marines when it came time to return to New Orleans. The pair desired to stay at Bayou St. John. Because they had been exposed to the hot sun for several weeks on the Mississippi River, the governor thought they would be "fit objects" for the pestilence. In concluding his message to their commanding officer, Claiborne interceded "with a view to the preservation of the lives of two faithful soldiers." While the two Marines may have avoided the fever, Claiborne reported to the Secretary of the Navy that two commissioned officers, two subalterns, and a third of the Marine privates fell to the fever. Fully aware of the dangerous climate, the Navy had assigned eight surgeons or acting surgeons and one surgeon's mate to Louisiana duty. The saffron scourge's deadly mystique in the region remained ingrained in the American military and naval rank and file for the rest of the century.[19]

Starting in the first decade of the century, American travel literature frequently discussed and often overstated the impact of the fever. During the fall of 1806, Irish traveler Thomas Ashe penned his observations on trade, religion, geography, and entertainment. The city attracted wanderers such as Ashe, who had served a short prison term in France for wounding a gentleman in a duel after seducing the man's sister. Ever on the move, Ashe sailed to North America. He gave the Americans credit for capitalizing on the city's commercial potential but greatly exaggerated the lethalness of the environs. The Irishman remarked that the lure of this river of plenty "lead[s] thousands into this country in search of a paradise, and they find a grave. On an average nine strangers die out of ten, shortly after their arrival in the city, and those who survive are of a shattered constitution and debilitated frame."[20]

Despite the influx of fevers, flooding, heat, and relentless mosquitoes, Americans from all walks of life understood the value of New Orleans as the key port on the Mississippi River. The Crescent City became the hub between the harvest of the Midwest, the Deep South, and the world. Cotton and sugar, and to a lesser degree hemp, wheat, hides, corn, tobacco, and pork left from the docks. European immigrants and travelers and African American slaves from the Upper South disembarked by the thousands. Amongst this mercantile hustling, the tiny mosquitoes lurked.[21]

When a merchant vessel arrived in port with ill occupants, regulations required the ship's master to fly a yellow flag, or jack. Consequently, the saffron scourge became known as yellow jack. But the dreaded fever was not the only mortal peril sailors faced. Scurvy, typhus, drowning, injuries, and ghastly wounds were just some the risks of the seafarers' trade. In the course of his lifetime, a mariner might work as a fisherman then sailor, and finally retire as a lighthouse keeper. These dangerous occupations were vital to the nation's commerce and defense and to generating revenue through tariffs.

In 1798, Congress passed an act to protect the health of mariners. The hazards of the occupation, separation from loved ones who normally offered health care, exposure to diseases, and the inclination of sailors to take risks were some of the reasons for this legislation. More important than the humanitarian reasons, however, was that the young nation had a vital economic interest in their collective livelihood. Shipmasters paid to custom collectors twenty cents a month from a sailing hand's pay, which maintained a maritime health service. A year later, the act was extended to cover naval seaman and Marines. This act also allowed for the hiring of physicians and the construction of hospitals in busy ports. Known originally as the Marine Hospital Service, under aegis of the Secretary of the Treasury, this agency eventually evolved to the U.S. Public Health Service.[22]

Keelboat men who polled boats down the Mississippi often found themselves alone in New Orleans during the sickly season after the cargo had been offloaded. The arduous trek and epidemic diseases took their toll on all seamen. River boatmen and oceangoing sailors who sailed into New Orleans were covered under this legislation even before Louisiana became a United States possession. Dr. William Bache, a grandson of Benjamin Franklin, was the first doctor to officially offer care to American mariners in the city. There was even serious discussion concerning the construction of a hospital. Despite the demand, a marine hospital was not constructed until the middle of the nineteenth century. Before the construction of the facility, customs authorities leased houses to serve as makeshift hospitals or sent the sick mariners to Charity Hospital.[23]

Long associated with the Sisters of Charity (in 1850, this community became the Daughters of Charity) was Charity Hospital. Found-

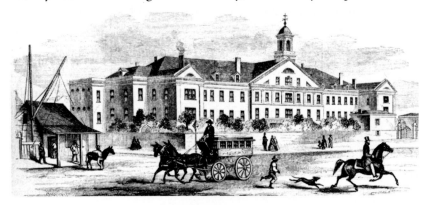

New Orleans Charity Hospital

ed in 1736 by French boat builder and mariner Jean Louis, it was originally known as Hospital of Saint John. Ravaged by hurricanes, Charity was saved in the 1790s by politico and speculator Andrés Almonaster y Roxas. After the Americans took control of Louisiana, the hospital fell under city and then state control. In the mid 1800s, the facility developed a national reputation as a teaching hospital and helped countless destitute yellow fever sufferers. The hospital survived fires, corruption, war, and neglect to be the training hospital for generations of doctors and nurses.[24]

The case of a former boatman and later sugar planter, Maunsel White, cared for by a black nurse serves as an example of one of the lucky keelboat men. In August 1801, White navigated a load of flour, tobacco, and pork down the Mississippi River only to contract fever in New Orleans. Decades later the boatman recalled that he fell into the immediate care of "Nanny, a great stout, strapping Negro woman, who wrapped me up in a sheet, took me up in her arms as one might take a baby." The nurse bathed and massaged White. She also cleaned his bedding, and attended her patient as she saw fit despite his feeble protests. In his weakened state, White mistook the portable bathtub for a coffin. Once in the tub, Nanny and another nurse proceeded to douse him with bucket after bucket of cold water. White lived at least forty-five years after the ordeal and later acknowledged his life-giving debt to Nanny and the doctors.[25]

In contrast to whites, few accounts have survived that provide details on how individual African Americans were treated for fever. Benjamin Latrobe did record that a slave named Maria was "suddenly seized with pains in her limbs, back and head, a dry skin and most violent fever." Dr. William Rogers "administered a strong cathartic and bled her. In 3 days her complaint vanished, leaving her only debilitated." Maria made a quick recovery. When a relatively high number of blacks died of the fever, physicians used that occurrence as an indication of a severe outbreak. Those outbreaks were also described as West Indian or true yellow fever epidemics.[26]

The Sisters of Charity and African American nurses were not the only residents known for their compassion and expertise. In 1804, when the fever threatened, Governor Claiborne relayed to James Madison that "I also observ'd with great pleasure, the Humanity of several Planters, who, by detaining at their Houses, some Americans destin'd for this City, have probably rescued them from sudden death!" Cumings, the river pilot, informed that there "are a number of other charitable institutions of respectable character; and when the yellow fever visits the city in the summer, the manner in which the inhabitants bestow charity, and nursing, and shelter, and medical aid to the sick is worthy of all praise."[27]

The confident citizens of Louisiana did not hesitate also to formulate their own regimen, having read and observed the dictates of physicians. These individuals administered strong medicines to themselves, family members, and servants. Judge Richard Claiborne prescribed for himself, wife, and children a preventative routine of confinement indoors, saltwater baths, and doses of calomel, that contained a compound with mercury, and jalap. Avoiding medicines that were almost as unnerving as the disease, other citizens correctly concluded that ingestion of harsh medicine did more harm than good.[28]

The economic burden of yellow fever pestilence was very difficult to measure, and the assumptions drawn by experts about the negative impact of an outbreak appeared in print often without supporting data. Nevertheless, by examining these statements and figures, one can get an understanding of the impact the illness had on the mindset of the survivors. In essence, the disease strangled business lifelines. Farmers, merchants, tradesmen, shippers, and financiers feared it and endeavored to avoid its stranglehold. Furthermore, if yellow fever erupted during economic recessions, such as it did in 1819 and 1822, the impact felt by farmers trying to get their depressed goods to market was doubly severe.[29]

The New Orleans pacesetters were hypersensitive to the city's chronic association with yellow fever. Newspaper editors bound their own futures to the city's prosperity and downplayed outbreaks. Out of frustration, Benjamin Latrobe "asked one of the Editors from what motive this omission arose; his answer was, that the principal profit of a newspaper arising from advertisements, the Merchants, their principal customers, had absolutely forbid the least notice of fever, under a threat their custom should otherwise be withdraw: thus sacrificing to commercial policy, the lives of all those who, believing from silence of the public papers, that no danger existed." City fathers supported the ruse. By not acknowledging the presence of an epidemic until weekly mortality reports indicated that there were more deaths from yellow fever than from any other cause, the local leaders allowed the fever to spread and delayed calls for help. The posed threat of epidemics fueled sharp verbal exchanges among politicians of various cities. State and municipal officials from Mississippi, Alabama, Texas, and Tennessee accused their counterparts in New Orleans of withholding information about the occurrence and extent of outbreaks. New Orleans newspapers countered that their competitors fanned inflammatory rumors to better their own monetary gain.[30]

In the 1820s, the Duke of Württemberg captured in words the vision Pitot foresaw and the menace of yellow fever. The German aristocrat concluded that "No trade center to me accommodates as many steamboats [and] no river system in the world furthers transportation by steamboat as does this. Under these conditions both trade and population would increase enormously if the climate and unhealthy situation did not disturb both. All strangers shun New Orleans from June to November to escape the deadly yellow fever. I arrived just at the end of such a terrible, all-ravaging epidemic."[31]

Noted architects Benjamin Henry Latrobe and his son, Henry S.B. Latrobe, both succumbed to yellow fever while working in New Orleans. This plaque in St. Louis Cemetery #1, New Orleans, commemorates their lives.

With New Orleans' growing reputation as a death trap, entertainers paused before accepting engagements in the Crescent City. In 1817, Noah Miller Ludlow, manager of the American Theatrical Commonwealth Company, had to convince his players that the yellow fever season had passed before the actors boarded the company's boat for New Orleans. Two years later, impresario James H. Caldwell had to coax his troupe from Virginia to New Orleans also because of fear of pestilence. Caldwell, a promoter in the same class as Phineas T. Barnum, did not convince everyone to take the trip. Despite the threat of fever, Caldwell kept New Orleans as the base of his theatrical operations for thirteen years. As for the great showman himself, Barnum's troupe visited New Orleans in the spring of 1838, but limited their engagement to a week before steaming northward on the *Ceres*. Yet the lure of antebellum New Orleans was persistent and Barnum returned to the city with the songstress Jenny Lind. "The Swedish Nightengale" gave a dozen concerts and added charity performances. Among other charities, Lind "appropriated $1,000 to the Sailor's Home in New Orleans." The Crescent City engagement was so successful that only in New York City did she give more performances.[32]

From 1817 to 1820, Benjamin Latrobe made some of the keenest observations concerning mosquitoes and yellow fever. Latrobe had first heard of the fever when he landed in Norfolk from Great Britain. He also saw firsthand the ravages of yellow jack in Philadelphia before taking a position in New Orleans. He assumed that the fever in New Orleans and Philadelphia were in essence the same disease. He described the stripes of a mosquito similar to the markings of the *A. aegypti*. He correctly concluded that the mosquitoes were attracted to dark colors, such as black hats. Latrobe also assumed that the mosquitoes "appear to have a means of discovering their food at a distance. In the day time, if you throw yourself upon a bed, or sit down, very few Muskitoes [sic], if any surround you. But in a quarter of an hour, they appear to discover you, and presently attack you in increasing swarms." Latrobe also observed the activity level of day-feeding mosquitoes that corresponded to the worst summer months of yellow fever epidemics. Latrobe saw that the females laid their eggs in water pitchers, wells, and rainwater cisterns and concluded that these were the insects that made life at home so miserable.

He also assumed that if cities installed a water system with pipes, the problem with the insects might be "considerably lessened" because the need for these open water receptacles would be eliminated.[33]

In 1817, Henry S.B. Latrobe died of yellow fever while employed by his father on a major water works project in New Orleans. Three years later, the observant Benjamin also fell victim to the scourge while pursing a business opportunity that promised long-term financial stability. Following the death of his father, John H.B. Latrobe left the U.S. Military Academy in his fourth year to help support his family.[34]

It is tragically ironic that the final resting place of yellow fever victims, New Orleans' distinctive cemeteries or "cities of the dead," actually contributed to the spread of the disease. Stagnant water filled permanent marble vases, urns, and other ornamentation, such as those at the base and to the right of this tomb, and created a prime breeding ground for *A. aegypti* mosquitoes.

Chapter Two

YELLOW FEVER IN THE ANTEBELLUM ERA, 1830s-1840s

We call him brave, who, when the trumpet's blare
Rang o'er the field of glory and of blood,
Went where the fight was deadliest, and stood
Where Duty placed him, with unaltered air. . . .[*]

Astute French commentator on American culture Alexis de Tocqueville could not resist inquiring about yellow fever during his day in New Orleans. Tocqueville queried resident Étienne Mazureau—was the fever "as much as a scourge here as supposed?" Mazureau responded that "they exaggerate the evil. My experience has taught me that of ten foreigners who live wisely and allow themselves no excesses of any sort, but two die." Given the required lifestyle restriction in a city known for its numerous excessive pleasures, Mazureau's conclusions were far from encouraging. Probably with that thought in mind, in 1831, British barrister Henry Tudor simply called the city "the head-quarters of Death!"[1]

One did not have to suffer with yellow fever to feel its lifelong psychological impact. Reverend Theodore Clapp, a transplant from the Northeast, tended to fever victims and their families for more than three decades. The Unitarian minister concluded that no acute disease was more painful and "there is none more shocking and repulsive to the beholder." The reverend devoted chapters of his memoirs to yellow fever and its aftermath. His memory was seared by the experience; the preacher confessed "Scarcely a night passes now, in which my dreams are not haunted more or less by the distorted faces, the shrieks, the convulsions, the groans, the struggles, and the horrors which I experienced thirty-five years ago."[2]

[*] Excerpt from "To The Howard Association of New Orleans," *Southern Literary Messenger* (October 1853): 642.

Reverend Theodore Clapp

Clapp thought this cyclical flow of fever and frost possessed "a wonderful sameness in the sombre [*sic*] realities of the sick room, the death struggle, the corpse, the shroud, the coffin, the funeral, and the tomb." In short, the fever was a ghastly but expected part of Louisiana life. In this romantic age, life was often hampered by debilitating ailments. Inquiries into a friend's health was more than an exchange of pleasantries. "Yellow Jack" became an anthropomorphic character that capriciously swept away the lives of entire families in one house and spared the neighbors. Natives were resigned to his visitations, and at the same time, wishfully expected most of the victims to be immigrants and visitors.[3]

Like the Latrobes, Abraham Oakey Hall sought his fortune in New Orleans. He was a young New Yorker and promising attorney who shared his observations of the exotic river town in the press. Publishers issued Hall's musings in book form, *The Manhattaner in New Orleans.* His New York-New Orleans connection had broader implications beyond his own life's story. There was a strong economic bond between the two cities, and numerous New Yorkers worked for Empire State firms operating in the Southern port. Consequently, New Yorkers became great contributors to the economic relief of yellow fever victims. Broader still is that this economic bond between Northern and Southern regions thrived despite the growing crisis just before the outbreak of the Civil War.[4]

Hall devoted an entire chapter of his book to yellow fever. He contracted the illness and asked his readers to imagine a "civil war is raging in the stomach, while the temples and the pulse beat a tatoo [*sic*] for the engagement. The head feels as if filled with molten lead which is burning the eyeballs. The back is like an unhinged door. . . . Daylight becomes a nuisance. The most fascinating of tongues loses its eloquence.

Ice is the greatest luxuries, and you would not sell the bit which covers your eyes (napkin enveloped) for place or money."[5]

Survivors of the mosquito-carried fever felt compelled to share their ordeal with others. In the late fall of 1834, John H.B. Latrobe overheard a conversation about yellow jack while steaming from New Orleans to Mobile. An unidentified passenger recounted his experience with the disease to a fellow traveler. Latrobe preserved the running commentary in his journal. The passenger recalled "He had first felt an approaching cold—he said. This made me prick my ears. Then after a day or two a tremendous headache—worse and worse thinks I—then a violent fever—and I began to count my pulse. Then pains in the back . . . limbs . . . and then delirium."[6]

The diminutive mosquitoes evoked as much verbal imagery as the much-larger alligators of the region. Travel literature, so popular in the Victorian era, abounded with vivid descriptions of the bloodthirsty pests. Much to the surprise of many travelers, the pest fed on humans from early spring to late autumn. In March 1830, Scottish lawyer James Stuart endured an attack of mosquitoes one evening. He recalled suffering "more from the bites of musquitos [*sic*] than I have before or since." When he chastised the maidservant for not instructing him on the proper use of "a musquito curtain," the maid smiled and replied that she left the curtain on the bed and thought Stuart had the wherewithal to use it. Stuart described the screening as "a tester . . . made of thick muslin, about the length and breadth of the bed, to which is attached a curtain four or five feet high, without openings at the sides" and folded beneath the bed cloths. The association of warm weather, mosquitoes, and yellow fever were so intertwined that it caused Stuart to pen the following remarkable, yet passing, statement concerning the connection between the fever and the mosquito: "The musquito curtain is universal among all classes of people here; indeed the loss of rest from the sting of the musquito has been frequently known to bring on the fever."[7]

As with other professions, the opportunity for financial success for physicians often overpowered the dread of the fever. In 1833, U.S. Army Surgeon Burton Randall attended to civilian patients not far from Fort Jackson. He reported to his brother Alexander in Annapolis that his fever-racked patients from New Orleans had been taken to a healthy atmosphere near Fort Jackson. Although the surgeon "felt exhausted at night both in mind and body," he still thought of the epidemic as a crossroads of his career.

Apparently Randall had an unsuccessful private practice and had fallen into debt. The epidemic, however, had killed many of the younger physicians in the city, and the older doctors would soon die of natural causes. Yet, the fear of more debt terrified Randall and he speculated that it would take two years before his private practice would make him self-sufficient. Admittedly, he "always felt more unhappy about the want of profitable patients than the disease that filled the streets."[8]

The 1840s were somewhat mild years for yellow fever. Serious epidemics only occurred twice in 1841 and 1847. In the former year roughly 1,500 people died and in the later year at least 2,300 succumbed to yellow jack. Soldiers returning from the Mexican War brought the fever to New Orleans and during the California Gold Rush some of the adventurers heading west contracted the fever. Enjoying this relative respite from the fever, sojourner Robert Baird remarked "I maintain and record the fact, that the unhealthiness of New Orleans is much exaggerated. No doubt the yellow fever visits it much oftener, and commits in more fearful ravages, than is at all desirable, but there are few places secure from the attacks of epidemics." The epidemics in the subsequent decade exploded Baird's cautious optimism.[9]

As New Orleans mushroomed into an international trading center, so did the need for a marine hospital. In 1848, a large hospital finally opened in McDonoughville on the west bank of the river, but inspection reports give the operation mixed reviews. The building was fine, but space was not used effectively and the location flooded. The facility and the grounds cost $123,000, a considerable sum compared to other marine hospitals.[10]

Another federal project that tried to monitor public health was the U.S. Army's study of the association between disease and certain atmospheric conditions. The army and navy both provided meteorological data for climatic/epidemical studies. Post and yard surgeons gathered the climatic records. Captains also oversaw the gathering of weather statistics in ships' logbooks. Spearheading this type of study was the Army Medical Department. In the 1840s, Army Surgeon General Samuel Forry compiled *The Climate of the United States and Its Endemic Influences.* The surgeon general examined humidity, wind currents, temperature, and barometric pressure. Expectedly, Forry found the gulf region the most lethal for soldiers. These studies by medical personnel such as Forry contributed to early systematic studies of weather in the United States.[11]

On the municipal level, the habit of burning articles that touched the dead was even integrated into funereal practices. In the warmer months, bodies were less likely to be laid out for public viewing, and in 1833, a city ordinance required burial of the dead within twenty-four hours to check the spread of disease. New Orleans is famous for its aboveground copings, wall vaults, and family and society tombs. The two-vault system allowed for the deceased family member to remain in a coffin for a year and a day before the remains were permanently deposited in the caveau section and mixed with the remains of family members. In this manner, loved ones could be buried in the same space. In the heat and humidity of Louisiana, bodies decomposed quickly. Sanitarians also recommended the use of lime to speed the process. Because of a fear of yellow fever, sextons burned the used coffins once the remains had been repositioned.[12]

In the nineteenth century, Southern cities lacked established infrastructures to battle infectious outbreaks. Instead, ad hoc public health committees formed as the fevers raged. City fathers depended on this volunteer effort and the spontaneous assistance of outsiders. There were standing volunteer groups, but they were small and selective. Older, well-established citizens in New Orleans joined the Good Samaritans, which visited the sick, hired nurses, and contributed funds. The Samaritans limited their group to

Howard officers finding the dead bodies of mother and child.

thirty members, while the Howard Association of New Orleans, organized in 1837, also called the Young Men's Howard Society, was more
active and served as a clearinghouse for food, medical supplies, and funds
donated from across the nation. William L. Robinson, a sugar broker and
a Howard Association member, typified the selfless spirit and preserved
the organization's deeds in his anonymously written autobiography, *The
Diary of a Samaritan*.[13]

The Howard Association served as a model for other philanthropic relief organizations for the rest of the South. Inspired by the Howard
Association, concerned citizens from fifteen cities in eight states created
their own groups based on the "peripheral action" of the New Orleans
association. The selfless example of John Howard, an eighteenth-century
English sanitarian and prison reformer, offered inspiration for the group's
name. Howard died of camp fever (probably typhus) in Russia during
his investigation of military hospitals. The Howards were young men
employed as grocers, merchants, importers, and clerks who took to the
streets to find those in need. Inauspiciously, during notable cholera and
yellow fever epidemics, notices appeared in the newspapers for members
to gather. They quietly organized the relief effort, often by wards, comforted the sick, and offered assistance to those families in need during the
worst of times. Forbiddingly, when unassuming notices appeared in print
that announced a meeting of the Howard Association, citizens assumed
that an epidemic was in full fury.[14]

The Howards faced heart-wrenching scenes when they ventured
into the abodes of fever sufferers. Yellow fever killed more adults than
children. Juveniles who survived the plethora of childhood ailments apparently suffered with milder cases of the fever or were better able to
endure yellow fever than their parents. A severe outbreak resulted in hundreds of orphans and widows. In the swirl of confusion, orphans lost
touch with their families, ethnicity, and even their own names. Others
fell victim to child snatchers who pressed the youngsters into service as
so-called apprentices. A bleak future, however, was not the destiny for
all of these ill-fated children. Kind neighbors often took them to their
hearth as one of their own offspring, and charitable, ethnic, and religious
based-organizations came to the rescue of many orphans.[15]

The yellow fever epidemics racked the city, crippled trade, and devastated families. Despite this horror, the leaders of Louisiana slowly learned from these viral attacks and responded to the needs of their community. Their efforts became the models for other state and municipal governments. Southern medical professionals listened intently when physicians of New Orleans speculated on the causes of, treatments of, and cures for the fever. Louisiana public health officials eventually developed procedures, equipment, and justifications for ship inspection, quarantine, and fumigation. Humane and sanitary societies emulated the altruism of New Orleans philanthropists and volunteers. And, from the struggle to free the city from the spasmodic grip of epidemics, the Louisiana State Board of Health emerged.

In the nineteenth century there were far fewer restrictions on the practice of medicine as compared to the twenty-first century and still fewer regulations that were enforced. Consequently, individuals could select from a host of healers. Doctors, pharmacists, conjurers, bleeders, patent medicine salesmen, and the well-intentioned lay persons espoused their favorite remedies. New Orleans' ever changing blend of cultures added another fluid dimension to this menagerie of medicine. Dr. Erasmus Darwin Fenner concluded, "In New Orleans may be seen the results of every imaginable course of treatment, from doing nothing at all up to the use of the most potent remedies in heroic doses and cases have recovered and died under all."[16]

Most Western medical practitioners believed that the human body was a "perfect, beautiful and harmonious instrument, each particle of matter having its own proper duty to perform." Ailments disrupted this keenly balanced alignment. Consequently, doctors and laymen addressed the negative symptoms of the disease by trying to counteract signs such as pain, high fever, and delirium. They employed medications and procedures that overpowered these negative manifestations. Humoral theory required the adjusting of four fluids or humors (blood, phlegm, yellow bile, and black bile) when the symptoms implied that there was an imbalance. This approach was well-entrenched in European medicine and drew upon the teaching of the ancient Greeks. Even in this broadly accepted supposition, however, there was room for interpretation.[17]

Medical professionals across the United States acknowledged the Herculean labors of Louisiana physicians to master yellow fever. The doctors of Louisiana issued pamphlets and monographs on their findings on curing and preventing the saffron scourge. Often these works contradicted each other and there were clashes among their collective egos. From the mountain of knowledge now amassed on yellow fever, it is easy to peer backwards and scoff at these physicians. Yet, a nineteenth-century doctor's point of view reveals a different perspective. If a caregiver had spent a lifetime fighting yellow fever and honestly concluded that he had obtained some great insight into the disease, was he not morally obligated to announce his lifesaving findings in the loudest possible terms? And despite their collective differences and their inability to control the yellow fever, the physicians of Louisiana were respected. Throughout the century, New Orleans physicians held important posts in all levels of medical organizations.

Physicians battling the fever lacked the diagnostic tests that are a part of modern medicine. Instead, doctors were compelled to monitor closely the symptoms and used what instruments were available to diagnosis an ailment. The French-educated Jean Charles Faget of New Orleans was one of the observant doctors who noted yellow fever patients had a slow, weak pulse despite a rising temperature. This observation called "Faget's sign" is an indication of the inflammation of the heart and remains "useful in differential diagnosis." He published his findings in French and English. One of his more notable publications was *Type and Specific Character of True Yellow Fever as Shown by Observations Taken with the Assistance of the Thermometer and Second Hand Watch*.[18]

Medical practitioners, especially in the early nineteenth century, regularly employed calomel, jalap, and quinine to combat yellow fever. Many of these treatments were very harmful. For more than 250 years, calomel, or mercurous chloride was "the most widely used of all mercurial drugs." Its variety of applications included use as a cathartic, diuretic, and expectorant. The mercury, however, blocks the body's ability to absorb water and nutrients. Other side effects included listlessness, stomach irritation, bleeding, and kidney and liver damage.[19]

From the early 1600s, jalap, a powdered root from Mexico, had been a part of Spanish medicine. It was administered as a mild cathartic and diuretic. Physicians and lay persons often administered quinine or cinchona religiously to check yellow jack and other fevers. Quinine was found in the powdered bark of various species of the cinchona trees of Peru. It was effective against the onslaught of malaria, but not against attacks of yellow fever.[20]

Bleeding reduced the "excess" blood, purges cleansed the bowels, and emetics induced vomiting. Peculiar to the South, some practitioners thought the heat of the region called for even more assertive approaches for some procedures to hasten the mending process. New Orleans physicians ran the gamut on the continuum concerning the validity of these methods. French physicians were more inclined to allow the body to heal itself. American doctors, such as oft-quoted Benjamin Rush of Philadelphia, took an opposite tack and applied a heroic regiment of treatments. Rush's supporters aggressively medicated, sweated, bled, blistered, and purged patients.[21]

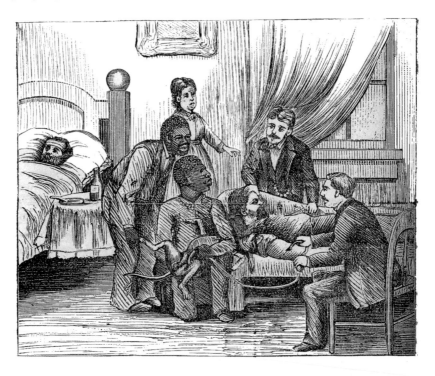

Mocking experimental yellow fever treatments, this satirical illustration from *Doctor Dispachemquic* by James Dugan shows a victim undergoing a blood transfusion with a dog.

The cuppers, bleeders, and phlebotomists practiced bloodletting (venesection). The procedure slowed the pulse and relaxed restless patients. Oddly, the practice was also used for broken bones, fainting, and spider bites. The bleeders extracted measured amounts of blood using specially designed surgical kits. Given the unstable mental state of yellow fever patients and the possibility for grievous accidents, a skilled bleeder was a valued member of the community. Extracting the prescribed amount of blood, with a minimum amount of pain and no spilling, was a surgical challenge. Phlebotomists pierced the skin with thumb or spring lances and drained the fluid into measured basins that monitored the flow. Cuppers shaved the skin, softened the epidermis with warm water, pierced the skin and covered the wound with a heated, bell-shaped cupping glass. This technique drew blood from the capillaries. Healers also harnessed the drawing power of leeches for venesection. Twenty to thirty leeches at one session extracted the blood. The leeches remained in place until they were gorged and then unleashed their grip on the patient.[22]

Medical advisories for travelers and seamen advocated wearing flannel, avoiding strong liquor except wine, maintaining a positive disposition, adhering to an "early to bed and early to rise" schedule, consuming meats and vegetables, exercising moderately in the early morning air, and drinking lemon juice with water and sugar. The guides also cautioned against constipation, sleeping too much, circulating night air, and walking in the rain and evening, eating too many sweet and juicy fruits, particularly pineapples, and too much physical exertion under intense sunlight.[23]

For middle-class Americans these suggestions were not only reasonable but also often followed and encouraged. Benjamin Latrobe passed along the following advice his son Henry "'Never sleep with your windows open. . . .' Be very temperate in your drink and fly to Pensacola in case of yellow fever." Likewise, Louisiana physicians supported moderation in diet, abstinence from alcohol, and avoidance of toiling in the direct sunlight.[24]

In contrast to the middle class, slaves and sailors were two groups of people that received second-rate medical care and had to work long and hard in a variety of dangerous conditions. Plantation overseers and shipmasters considered medical fees expensive and doctors were not always accessible. Cookbook-like manuals served as self-help advisories. These directions often accompanied medicine chests for duty at sea or the toils on plantations. Similar to the European immigrant guides, New England surgeons and apothecaries issued these self-help books to ship-masters, sailors, overseers, and travelers in "sickly climates" or "hot climates." Dr. Danforth P. Wight's guide for yellow fever prescribed bleeding in conjunction with calomel, jalap mixed with molasses, and sponge baths of vinegar and water. Opium could be used to check the ill effects of mercury, and blistering was to counter vomiting.[25]

Most African Americans were not allowed to practice a moderate lifestyle but the race's resistance to yellow fever was a puzzle that was never resolved. Perplexed by this situation, Dr. Bennet Dowler could not determine if black resistance to the fever was the result of skin color, a permanent factor in their constitution obtained from the climate of Africa, or an inherited feature peculiar to the race. Blacks worked in the hot sun. Slaves harvested crops, buried their dead, held secret meetings, and visited family members all at night. Well aware of blacks' resistance to fever, Dr. Samuel Cartwright thought only black stevedores should handle the cargoes at the wharves. Whites viewed slaves as creatures that lusted for the same base pleasures as sailors. The dancing, singing, and playing of music inspired by African rhythms shocked whites such as Benjamin Latrobe and reinforced this view of the sensual nature of slaves. Yet, black resistance to yellow fever was universally acknowledged.[26]

A careful analysis of the mortality statistics of the epidemic supports the observation that blacks were far less likely to die from yellow fever. Even those African Americans who arrived in New Orleans as part of the domestic slave trade apparently had a natural resistance to the fever. Marched in coffles or shipped from the upper South, many of these individuals were in their teens and older. Therefore, they were less likely to have been exposed to yellow fever coming from rural areas or from cities such as Richmond or Norfolk. Even with the occasional outbreak of the disease in the upper South, again where the slaves were less likely to have been exposed to yellow fever as children, the mortality figures indicated far fewer blacks died of the disease.[27]

One medical explanation offered by a Mississippi doctor for the low mortality among children of all races and adult African Americans was that African Americans and children were far less complex and not capable of comprehending the devastation that an epidemic could bring. Consequently, they were not likely to worry themselves into contracting the fever. Reports frequently commented on this characteristic of the disease. Following the epidemic of 1873, *Scientific American* noted in Louisiana "that no single colored person took the yellow fever, and they rarely ever take it unless it is fiercely epidemic."[28]

What baffled nineteenth-century physicians remains somewhat of a mystery. Not only did fewer blacks die of the disease, far fewer appeared to contract the fever, and those African Americans who did fall ill displayed milder symptoms. A modern study conducted in the Ashanti region of Ghana suggested the possibility for low morbidity may be the result of "the observed presence of other predators which prey on *A. eygypti* larvae in the study areas, the low larval indices and the low man-vector contact rates recorded as well as the high prevalence of Group B antibodies found in the blood of the population of the region may be contributory to the paucity of yellow fever in the Ashanti region." Perhaps the presence of these Group B antibodies also protected slaves in the Americas.[29]

With this natural protection, African American women nurses were in high demand during outbreaks. The combination of extensive experience and resistance to the fever allowed them to command high compensation for their labor and "although their fees might run as high as $10 per day, they often gave their services gratuitously to those whom they considered respectable but were unable to pay." Some of black nurses journeyed as part of a relief party to other Southern cities stricken with fever. In addition, African American hacks, draymen, and carters provided the much needed city transportation that moved the physicians, volunteers, and the bodies of the deceased to the cemeteries. Resistance to the fever empowered slaves and they knew how to use the matter of survivability to their psychological advantage. Consider the mental state of Capt. Thomas Hamilton when he learned from a dour female slave that three men had perished in the captain's current lodgings and the women had laid out two bodies for burial on the table in Hamilton's room.[30]

African Americans not only nursed the afflicted. Talented stone masons, such as Prosper and Florville Foy, carved the ornate tombs that housed the earthly remains of the deceased. And in contrast to noble nurses and skilled masons, African American convicts, plied with strong drink, buried the dead. Whether laborers or craftsmen, men or women, voluntary or compulsory, African Americans played vital roles when the white denizens of New Orleans suffered with yellow fever.[31]

Not all of the slaves sought to help their white masters in time of crisis. In 1804, 1837, and 1853, rumors of revolts surfaced in the midst of epidemics. In mid-June 1853, white citizens were more focused on the rumblings of an uprising than the sporadic cases of yellow fever. Certainly, many slaves saw this a golden opportunity for a mass uprising. Juxtaposition against the near panic the disease caused in whites and their exodus from the city was the opportunity for freedom the virus offered to slaves. The concern about the alleged revolt was real enough that the governor mustered the state militia.[32]

While epidemics could be a boon for African Americans, according to Dr. Joseph C. Simmonds, from 1846 to 1850, the city suffered losses of almost $45.5 million. The trade journal *De Bow's Review* drew upon a local medical journal to refute the city's reputation "as a perfect charnel house" claiming that other cities had similar mortality rates and the statistics needed to take into account the city's tremendous transient population. In spite of the campaigning of city leaders, the view of New Orleans as a "whited sepulchre" remained.[33]

Despite the fever's reputation, associates from the Northeast arrived to represent large and small businesses in the New Orleans. Many of the Americans and immigrants did not establish permanent residency in New Orleans. If the American business associate was married, his family might remain at home. Employees often returned to a firm's base of operations in New York, Baltimore, Boston, or Philadelphia during the sickly season. As transplants, these field representatives were part of the largest body of non-native American residents in New Orleans. Similarly, in the 1840s, more than 160,000 passengers disembarked in New Orleans but relatively few settled in the city. Local sources estimated the floating population to be between 40,000 to 50,000 people. In contrast to the transients, some of the clerks, tradesmen, and rising merchants who survived the fever and married into established Louisiana families made major contributions to financial, civic, and educational institutions.[34]

Selected individuals demonstrate varying migratory patterns. A few years after his arrival in New Orleans in 1822, Jewish merchant Solomon Soher formed a dry goods partnership. Soher also invested in steamboats. He married Miriam Andrews, but it appears his wife never resided in New Orleans. The couple's three children were all born during the spring in New York City. A sampling of 125 Jewish businesses operating between 1840 and 1866 reveals that fifty-two establishments closed without cause, but a number of the unidentified closings were linked to the Panic of 1857 and yellow fever epidemics.[35]

In a like manner, Irish-born Pennsylvanian James Robb arrived on the levee with just a few hundred dollars. In ten years he amassed a fortune through banking, utilities, and mercantile partnerships. He moved in the highest social circles and held numerous political offices. In contrast to the Soher family, the Robb family paid dearly for their ties to New Orleans. In 1855, Louisa Robb, a daughter, died of the fever. Clearly, the Robb family had the means to leave the city during the summer, but may have remained in town because James Robb was ill at the time.[36]

Like Soher and Robb, two adventurers to antebellum New Orleans were newspapermen Walt Whitman and his younger brother Jefferson. In February 1848, the pair arrived in the Crescent City from New York. In a feeble attempt to assure his mother that the "alarm about the yellow fever" was exaggerated, Jefferson relayed that "It does not come but once in three or four years, and last season it was very hard and killed a great many persons. . . . Besides it is a great humbug, most every one in our office has had (some of them have had it twice) and got well. It is caused mostly (I think all of it) by the habit of the people, they never meet a friend but you have to go drink and such loose habits."[37]

Apparently it did not occur to Jefferson Whitman that if bad habits caused an individual to contract the fever, he had informed his mother that the city was brimming with nefarious people. Also, if his coworkers had allegedly contracted the fever twice, they were a particularly suspect group of men. Whatever the cause of the fever, the Whitman brothers did not stay long in the city. In late May, Walt Whitman and his employer clashed, and the brothers returned in Brooklyn. Given the impact the Civil War had on Walt Whitman's body of work as a poet, one must wonder about the sway yellow fever epidemics may have had on the impressionable poet.

HISTORY

OF THE

YELLOW FEVER

NEW ORLEANS,

DURING THE

SUMMER OF 1853.

WITH SKETCHES OF THE

SCENES OF HORROR

WHICH OCCURRED DURING THE EPIDEMIC:

DESCRIPTIONS AND BEAUTIFUL ILLUSTRATIONS OF

CHARITY HOSPITAL, AND THE PUBLIC CEMETERIES,

AND ESPECIALLY OF

POTTER'S FIELD,

AND THE METHOD OF BURYING THE DEAD IN CYPRESS SWAMP.

TO WHICH IS ADDED THE NAMES OF ALL PERSONS WHO CONTRIBUTED TO THE FUNDS OF THE

HOWARD ASSOCIATION,

IN ALL PARTS OF THE UNITED STATES, AND THE AMOUNT CONTRIBUTED BY EACH PERSON,

WITH THE OFFICIAL REPORT

OF THE DOINGS OF THAT SOCIETY, &c.,

BY A PHYSICIAN OF NEW ORLEANS,

WHO WAS PRESENT DURING THE FATAL EPIDEMIC OF 1853.

PHILADELPHIA AND ST. LOUIS,
PUBLISHED BY C. W. KENWORTHY,
1854.

The Howard Association cared for more than 11,000 yellow fever patients in 1853.

Chapter Three

PESTILENTIAL HORRORS IN THE CAPITAL OF THE COTTON KINGDOM, 1850s

The sun sinks down o'er each death-crowded street,

Whilst dread, delirious screams the hearing greet;

Night settles o'er with awe and tear and gloom.

What means yon glaring blaze, yon cannon's boom?

Ha! Victory's tokens for the conqueror Death!

*Who slays his thousands by the fever's breath!**

By the middle of the century the shadow of pestilence described by Claiborne, the Latrobes, and European visitors had become an international image. *The Illustrated London News* declared that the city was "Built upon a site that only the madness of commercial lust could have ever tempted men to occupy—a huge swamp at the mouth of the Mississippi—it subjects all but its natives and negro [*sic*] inhabitants to a process of acclimation; under which ordeal a large proportion of them perish." Cavorting with that "commercial lust," foreign governments, including Great Britain, established twenty-nine consulates in the city.[1]

Great cotton shipments, cataclysmic epidemics, the pending Civil War, the liberation of the slaves, the vicious struggles for power, and economic decline all defined the period. New Orleans was both the most important city in the South and the sickliest city in America. The debates that involved states rights, regional peculiarities, and the morality of slavery became intertwined with Northern reaction to the epidemics and relief efforts. The sectional differences became so pronounced that a

* Poem stanza is part of an unfinished poem written by a physician and fever victim in Bennet Dowler, *Tableau of the Yellow Fever of 1853, Topographical, Chronological, and Historical Sketches, The Epidemics of New Orleans Since Their Origin in 1796 Illustrative of the Quarantine Question* (New Orleans, 1854), 62.

writer in *Harper's New Monthly Magazine* concluded that "every climate must have its distinctive race; and though Yankee blood can brave much of danger, it can never successfully combat the pestilential vapors of New Orleans."[2]

Antebellum New Orleans had unique characteristics that highlighted it as the premier city in Dixieland. In 1860, the population stood at about 180,000 residents. No other Southern city came close to that number. This populace supported a world-renowned theater, the opera, and musical concerts. As a port, New Orleans rivaled New York City. The local U.S. Customs Office boasted more than 220 employees. Stevedores loaded millions of cotton bales on outward-bound ships while tens of thousands of immigrants landed annually on the docks. Intertwined in this pulsating metropolis were the horrible specter of epidemics and the pending shadow of war. From 1849 to 1858, between twenty to twenty-five thousand people died of yellow fever in New Orleans.[3]

Arriving in New Orleans in November, Lady Emmeline Stuart Wortley took the advice of a maid and did not deploy the mosquito netting before her evening repose. As a result, mosquitoes feasted on the lady. Exasperated, Wortley's diatribe against the insect continued for two pages, calling them the "the most ubiquitous little monsters in existence." She went on to complain that "in the day time it is hateful enough, but at night far worse. However, at night one has the happy resource of the 'bars' as they call the net apparatus." As Wortley inadvertently illustrated, *A. eygypti* day-feeding mosquitoes, although not as aggressive as its nocturnal cousins, did not always have to contend with netting to obtain a blood meal.[4]

In their published travel log, Jane and Marion Turnbull recalled that African American draymen dressed their mules "in white or checked trousers and smock frocks, and some even had awnings stretched over their backs, to protect them from the heat of the sun and mosquitoes." For visitors not appareled like draft animals, mosquito bars were "a most necessary appendage." In addition, the couple warned that the mosquitoes "abound in New Orleans" and were "very partial to foreigners." In contrast, long time resident and architect Thomas K. Wharton described the pesky insects in muted terms such as "mischievous" or "something more than even we are accustomed to." As travelers quickly learned, to defend against this airborne onslaught, mosquito bars or netting were as much a part of a decent night's rest as a glass of warm milk.[5]

The yellow fever epidemics in the 1850s were among the most fearful in the city's history and the attack in 1853 was the worst outbreak to strike New Orleans. From May to November, mortuary statistics revealed that more than 12,100 people died. At least 9,000 were victims of yellow fever. And more than 3,500 and 2,300 were Irish and German immigrants, respectively. The following year 2,500 people died, and in 1855, 2,670 residents perished. There were minor outbreaks for two years, before another bad epidemic in 1858 that consumed 4,855 lives. Following these medical disasters, outraged citizens clamored for major improvements. These tirades had a limited effect and did not prevent the outpouring of arguments about yellow fever and the promotion of alleged cures.[6]

In the grips of an epidemic much of the normal commercial activity was muffled or ceased. Only the graveyards, saloons, and hospitals were busy. At cemeteries the laborers arranged hastily made coffins like crates in a warehouse. The sextons hired temporary labor and paid them handsomely to inhume the mounting accumulation of coffins and bodies. To check the reeking smell of the dead and protect against the fever, the laborers wore poultices and "Nose bags of camphour and ordorous

Mid-nineteenth-century New Orleans cemetery scene

[*sic*] spices." Alcohol fortified the gravediggers with liquid courage as they toiled and cracked "jokes in the horrid atmosphere." Still, there was a shortage of diggers, so friends and family members buried their own kinfolk. Victims died every hour, and the grisly business in the cemeteries continued around the clock. In 1853, approximately 2,000 people were buried in each of five different cemeteries, oftentimes in shallow, mass graves. Authorities pressed chain gangs of African Americans into service and appealed to citizens to send them food while the convicts buried the dead.[7]

This apocryphal scene was oft repeated in the clutches of an epidemic. Many of the city's inhabitants left before the start of the summer. Others timed their flight at the first signs of sickness. The docks remained inactive because the bounty of cotton and other crops had yet to be sent to market. During particularly bad outbreaks, the shipments were delayed or routed away from the city. Tar was burned and the militia fired artillery pieces to disrupt the deadly miasma thought to be blanketing the city. The report of the guns unnerved the sufferers so it was not a common practice but when it occurred, it only added to the sense of apocalyptic doom.[8]

More than nine thousand people died in New Orleans during the 1853 epidemic. The burying of the dead was carried out far into the night by the glow of torches and lanterns.

As the angel of death gathered souls, some fever victims remained remarkably stoic. John Freeman received a letter from his brother that described the passing of the young Thomas Pugh. The brother relayed that the "family did not realize his danger till the day before his death. His father then told him that he must die. Wh [*sic*] he bore more calmly than any of the others. He had them called in servants & all & took leave of each one separately and expressed his readiness to die. His mother prayed & talked with him a great deal and I have every reason to think he sleeps with Jesus." Hearing such accounts may have been part of the reason that John Freeman joined the Episcopal priesthood.[9]

Along with victims such as Pugh, the great swell of unacclimated immigrants fell to the fever. Tragically, thousands of Irish peasants of the potato famine found themselves in another death struggle in their new homeland. It was cruel irony that that this was not the first time that Irish famine migrants had experienced such an ordeal. The starvation in Ireland sparked widespread outbreaks of dysentery, scurvy, relapsing fever, and typhus. The latter two diseases, carried by lice, were also known respectively as black fever and yellow fever, although they were not related to the viral, tropical yellow fever. Compounding the tragedy was the

A crowded cemetery near the Metairie Race Course as it appeared during the 1853 epidemic.

belief by American citizens that the immigrants died of fever because of a predisposition aggravated by factors such as "reckless and intemperate living habits," unsanitary living conditions, and laboring in the heat.[10]

As waves of immigrants departed Europe, publishers issued informational pamphlets, broadsides, and self-help books. Laymen medical guides abounded. One of those translated German guides acknowledged that "physicians vary in their opinions." Nevertheless, the authors advised early bleeding, two to eight cups depending on the constitution of the patient, calomel, castor oil laced with molasses to prevent vomiting, and a laxative of cooling salts. Leeches could be applied to the head and stomach. Care also included keeping the patient cool and offering refreshments of sugar water, vinegar, and lemon juice. Warm beverages were to be avoided.[11]

Illuminated by flambeaux, brave humanitarians and physicians visited immigrants at all hours of the night when the fever struck. The sickrooms had a peculiar smell associated with the fever. Elsewhere, volunteers found nursing children pulling at their mothers' breasts, but the women did not respond. Watching the horror from the shadows, human vultures darted from their cover and preyed on the dead and stole their worldly possessions.[12]

Children returning home with coffins for other members of their family.

In the deadly clutches of a fever epidemic, New Orleans mirrored the outskirts of Hades. Barrels of pitch might burn on street corners, and the clothing and bed linens of the departed were torched. Families marked the passing of loved ones by adorning doorways with black, lavender, or white crepe paper. Posted notices marked closed businesses and funeral announcements personalized the mortality statistics. The hearses and hacks clacked down the empty alleys. "Coffin rumbled after coffin; the funeral columns defiled almost constantly for months from every street." Survivors followed hearses. Smaller, white coffins did not require hearses, as they were cloaked in satin with ribbons and carried by surviving children.[13]

The seasonal death toll faded in the late fall. The first frosts were the natural portent that yellow jack's grip was weakening as the female mosquitoes were not hunting for a blood meal. The frost was nothing short of a godsend. Ever watchful, Thomas Wharton recorded in his journal on November 6, 1858, that "After a long delay, the frost came unmistakably last night, and the grass was well crisped early in the morning. . . . The scourge of the summer is vanishing rapidly." Later in that same month, Wharton noted a "Strong white frost in the night."[14]

Almost 3,050 patients were treated at New Orleans Charity Hospital during the 1853 epidemic, 1,750 of which died.

43

New Orleans pathologist John Harrison was one of the physicians who pontificated on yellow fever. In a paragraph in his article titled "Remarks on Yellow Fever," Harrison assured the reader that he had treated many cases of yellow fever at Charity Hospital and had performed "several hundred post mortem examinations." Harrison noticed that mosquito bites on the deceased "become dark and livid." While he did not specify if the corpses he examined were his former patients, the doctor stressed he had "experienced the disease in my own person." This familiarity with the scourge positioned Louisiana physicians in the vortex of a host of yellow fever controversies.[15]

John Harrison declared that of "all the diseases which afflict [the] human race, there is none that requires more unremitting care and attention on both physician and nurse, than yellow fever." He conducted numerous autopsies on the remains of yellow fever victims. This experience gave him a unique insight into the impact of the virus and the treatments on the major organs of the human body. Harrison admonished his

Volunteers, neighbors, and friends were often shocked to learn that the fever had swept away entire families.

peers to treat the man, not the disease. In other words, watch the symptoms closely and proceed accordingly. Harrison incorrectly assumed that calomel was no longer advanced in the 1850s and thought its application a sign of desperation. Harrison was not an advocate of bleeding sufferers or offering stimulants and narcotics. Still, the pathologist was very much a part of his times when he prescribed to the value of quinine, purgatives, and sponge baths.[16]

Dr. Eramus Darwin Fenner's history of the epidemic of 1853 included his medical regimen and selected medical case histories that demonstrate the techniques and medicines applied in support of the medical theories. Fenner advocated sponge baths of vinegar or whiskey and water, calomel, mild enemas, and bloodletting as part of a regimen of cures. He also supported the use of quinine. When quinine failed as a cure in 1853, he countered that the fever was particularly malignant and that thoughtless physicians misapplied quinine.[17]

Excerpts from Fenner's studies show the methods used to counteract symptoms and to adjust the body's disoriented humors. An unidentified doctor aggressively treated a New Orleans butcher by having "him copiously bleed" and by giving him "an active cathartic," croton oil, and a strong enemata. Croton oil was pressed from a triangular-shaped nut. The nut had a peculiar smell "and an acrid and hot taste." It was used as a powerful purgative, causing "irritation and inflammation of the skin, followed by a pustular" eruption. The combination of fever and irritants caused the patient to regurgitate "black matters." Popular opinion claimed the black vomit foretold of certain death, but the butcher survived the disease and the treatment and was "discharged as cured on the twelfth day." Scotsman John Allen, a two-year resident of city, worked on the levee. After Allen contracted the fever, the attending physician had the patient cupped, purged, and then sent to Charity Hospital. At the hospital, physicians applied a blister to his stomach and "and gave him but little medicine but had him carefully nursed." Allen returned home after eight days.[18]

Those experts who concluded that microscopic agents were the cause of the fever presumed that infectious particles or fomites of yellow fever infested the remains of the dead, certain cargoes, mail, and clothing. The disease was transferred when these inanimate carriers were shifted from one location to the next. The people of New Orleans were accused of reusing the garments and linen of fever victims. There was, however, a conscious effort to burn these items and fumigate the quarters of the dead with sulfur, lime, and other chemicals. Following the death of her husband, Mary Elizabeth Latrobe "had some nitric acid in the house which [she] burned as soon as possible . . . gathered all the clothes, [and] sent them away." In 1854, the authors of a report observed that "Abundant evidences [*sic*] exist of its transmissibility from one diseased town to another, by persons and fomites."[19]

Dr. Edward H. Barton of New Orleans was the strongest advocate of the link between the weather (heat, ventilation, filth, and moisture) and yellow fever. He boldly dismissed the proposition of harmful microbes, and instead, closely monitored dew points and humidity. Sanitarians supported Barton's view linking filth and weather as critical ingredients for the fever. Opponents, and there were many in New Orleans, thought Barton over-emphasized the importance of climatic forces.[20]

Fenner, Harrison, and Barton were just a trio of the medical practitioners in New Orleans. In the 1850s, the city directories listed more than 120 physicians and a hundred apothecaries. Some of the physicians owned or were associated with the drug stores. A. Oakey Hall quipped that "The chances of a patient's recovery vary with the degrees of favor his physician enjoys at the shop of the apothecary. If he have a nephew or a cousin in the drug line, the patient is a dead man from the second day." Hall's slight was right on the mark. At times, doctors and druggists conspired to overcharge for medicines, and some physicians took kickbacks from druggists.[21]

For numerous reasons, many individuals developed their own methods of "curing" yellow fever. The working class did not always have the monetary means to call for a doctor, so home cures had to suffice. Understandably, some citizens lacked faith in the mainstream medical practitioner's ability, and everyone had access to the same medicines without acquiring a doctor's prescription. In addition, the public saw that the medical profession did not fully grasp the forces that created epidemics. American self-reliance manifested itself in medical texts and kits for laymen. When all else failed, hundreds of patent medicine barkers hawked their tonics to a desperate and gullible public.

These arguments on the cures and prevention could overwhelm hapless patients, many who did not respect doctors in general and were new to the country and unfamiliar with the dreaded fever. Packets for New Orleans departed Europe often in the cooler months to avoid the turbulent North Atlantic Ocean and the sickly season in the South. On the down side, the trip took longer than following the more direct passage to the northeastern United States, and new arrivals were weakened by typhus, typhoid fever, and the long journey. Those immigrants that remained in New Orleans were no less vulnerable to the fever when the disease struck the following summer. In 1853, nearly 38,000 immigrants arrived. The devastation to the immigrant population was so severe that public health officials recommended that transporting immigrants during the warmer months was "immortal and unchristian, and that our safety, as much as theirs, requires that they should not be allowed to enter the port, where death awaits them."[22]

Landladies, employers, and family members attended to the sick but the burden of caring for fever patients taxed even people with the best of intentions. Thus, many Irish and German immigrants were sent to the overcrowded Charity Hospital as a last resort. Many even died en route to the hospital. Eliza Lacy was among the hundreds of new arrivals who landed in the hospital. The young Irish woman arrived in the fall of 1852 and resided in Algiers, on the west bank of the Mississippi River. During the epidemic of the following year, she was admitted to Charity Hospital and suffered a fortnight before she died. She hemorrhaged from her mouth and her stomach (where she had been blistered). All told, in 1853, Charity Hospital handled 3,052 cases of fever, many like Lacy's, of which 1,765 perished.[23]

The endeavors of Northerners to alleviate the suffering caused by yellow fever were not entirely altruistic. The two regions had strong business ties that were lashed by shipping lines, railroads, and river commerce. A sharp economic downturn precipitated by an epidemic in the Southern states had a rippling effect across the nation. Northeastern banking and trade interests operated in New Orleans. Much of the South's cotton was exported from New York to Liverpool. The fever harmed many interested parties. Furthermore, Northerners noticed troubling similarities among the conditions in their respective cities and New Orleans. All attempts

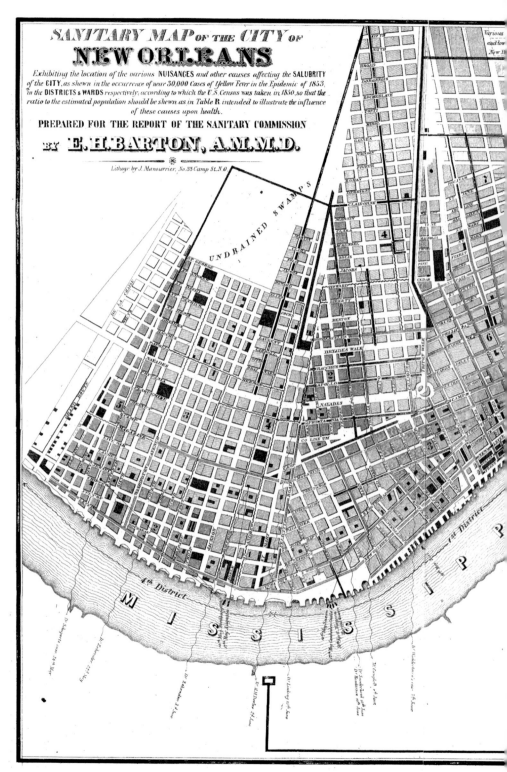

Dr. Edward H. Barton's map of suspected causes of the 1853 epidemic.

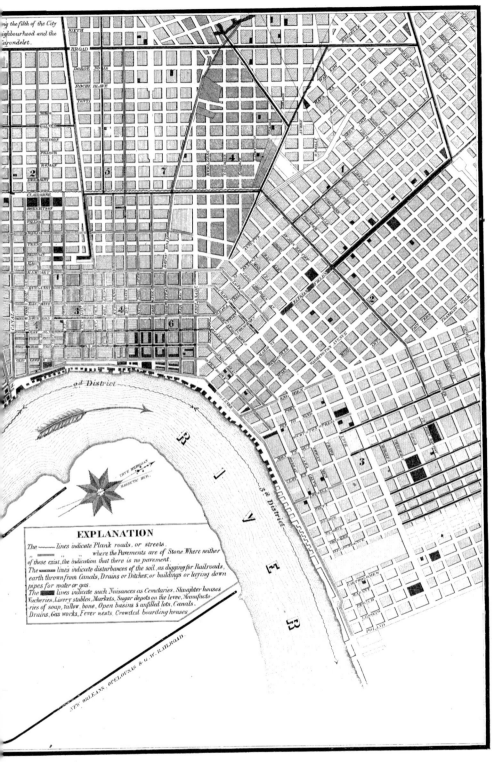

and capital sunk into fighting and preventing outbreaks might one day pay dividends. The editor of New York City's *Harper's New Monthly Magazine* warned "the pestilence will come upon us as a thief in the night, and while it steals away our life and our joy, we shall impotently wonder why we did nothing to help ourselves."[24]

During the New Orleans epidemic of 1853, James Gordon Bennett's *New York Herald* accused a Philadelphia paper of misrepresenting the monetary contributions made by the citizens of Manhattan. According to the *Herald*, *Philadelphia North American* reprinted the contributions given in relief of pestilence, reducing the New York contribution by fifteen thousand dollars and adding three thousand dollars to the actual amount contributed by Philadelphians. In addition, the *Herald* claimed the alteration was "done for the express purpose of lowering the city of New York in the estimation of our Southern fellow-citizens and raising Philadelphia."[25]

Non-residents that survived the fever were quick to relate the ordeal to loved ones back home. In many ways the plight of the Thomas family represented the potential ruin that venturesome New England entrepreneurs faced in moving to the city. Henry, Sr., his namesake, and other family members headed from Connecticut to Louisiana. In 1851, William O. Thomas, wife Jane S.P. Thomas, and their immediate family joined the clan and settled in the Garden District. Two years later, the city's worst epidemic engulfed the family. Despite the attentive care of William, brother George H. Thomas died of the fever at the end of July. Five-year-old Willie Thomas (son of William and Jane) died on the first day of August. Willie's mother, Jane Thomas, succumbed on midnight two days later. Having lost his wife, son, and brother, William attempted to flee but died of the fever at the end of August in Cincinnati. By the 1860s, most of the surviving family members had left New Orleans and had returned to New England.[26]

Other than their decision to remain in the city during the summer, there is no indication that the lifestyle of the Thomases made them any more susceptible to the fever than other New Englanders. Nonetheless, this was an era when predisposition to illnesses was a common assumption. In this environment it was easy to understand why people thought mariners were likely candidates to contract yellow fever. Seafarers toiled day and night in all types of weather conditions. They experienced stress caused by separation from their families. Furthermore, their reputation for enjoying earthly pleasures in port was well established. Therefore, it was no surprise that sailors, regardless of their race and background, suffered from yellow jack. To avoid the seaman's fate, according to nineteenth-century thought, a person needed to demonstrate self-control. Excesses drained individuals of their strength and natural ability to fight infections. Moderation lessened the severity or eliminated the chances of contracting diseases such as yellow fever and cholera. Often times when a respected immigrant or native did die in an epidemic their obituary was certain to a point out the deceased's virtures.[27]

The lithographic images on the cover of the sheet music illustrated the elegy of the demise of a youthful New Englander in New Orleans. One view showed a lad with a bundle on a hilltop gazing into a valley. The center image revealed a deathbed scene with an elderly lady and attending physician. Surrounding these images are angels and a cemetery far more reminiscent of the famed resting place of Mt. Auburn in Cambridge, Massachusetts, than the vaults and mausoleums found in southern Louisiana. Considering that a Boston publisher issued the sheet music, this comes as no surprise. The story that inspired this ballad involved a young man from Maine who journeyed to the South to make his fortune, but like so many others fell to the fever. Shortly after the youth's death, an empathizing woman sought to kiss the young man "for his mother." The middle stanza best represents the lament:

> Let me kiss him for his Mother,
> What though left alone a stranger here;
> She has loved him as none other,
> I feel her blessing near.
> Though cold that forms lies sleeping,
> Sweet angels watch around;
> Dear friends are near thee weeping;
> Oh! lay him gently down.[28]

In the aftermath of these epidemics, there was tremendous public demand for improvements. For instance, sanitarians insisted that dis-

"Let Me Kiss Him for His Mother" (c. 1859) is the title of a ballad written by John P. Ordway. The song chronicled the true story of a young man from Maine who journeyed to New Orleans to make his fortune. Instead, the lad died of yellow fever among strangers. A sympathetic older woman gave him a last kiss as his surrogate mother.

eases spontaneously generated from the fetid filth, standing water, heat, and rotting animal remains around the city. Therefore, paved streets, enforced sanitation procedures, clean drinking water, and a unified sewage system were the solution to eliminate yellow fever and other diseases. In conjunction with these man-made breeding conditions, public health supporters pointed an accusatory finger at turned earth, meteorological conditions, and swamplands that created miasmata able to veil the city in a deadly shroud. In the mid-1800s, microorganisms, known as animalcules, were not seriously considered as the cause. Rudolph Matas, one of the greatest figures of medicine in Louisiana history, surmised that of "all the influences that retarded the development of modern concepts of the infectious and epidemic diseases, the belief in spontaneous generation of the these epidemics out of 'miasms' emanating from decomposing inorganic or dead organic matter, in conjunction with physical, chemical, climatic and other cosmic forces, was the greatest hindrance."[29]

On the state level, one agency that developed as a direct result of the yellow fever epidemics was the Louisiana State Board of Health. The board was the nation's first permanent state public health organization. Organized in 1855, the agency struggled in its early years, faded during the Civil War era, but reemerged after the war. Many of the city's and state's public health associates, including Joseph Holt and Joseph Jones, became international leaders in the evolving fields of quarantine management and public health.[30]

Investigations into the source of yellow fever epidemics invariably fused shipping and filth with the disease. Some physicians believed that heat, moisture, and certain unhealthy shipboard conditions spawned the fever. Opponents of this view did not refute the fever's presence on board ships but argued only that the fever germs or fomites were generated by in the city's own cesspools before infected vessels arrived. Despite notable theories to the contrary, the finger pointing at ships and their occupants was regular practice. The 1853 epidemic was linked to the *Augusta* from Bremen. An Irish immigrant, reportedly one of the first victims, may have contracted the fever from a nearby ship. Not everyone, however, feared the filth and the fomites. Physicians such as M. Morton Dowler debunked the "filth theory" advocated by sanitarians. Dowler warned that the clamor against the dregs found on board ships and in the streets was a "crusade against filth, on the yellow fever basis, go to expending millions of the public money, and devouring the commerce of New Orleans" to no positive end.[31]

As medical practitioners argued about the source of the fever, organizations such the Howard Association struggled to soften the blow of personal tragedies in the wake of an epidemic. In 1853, the association assumed the care for ninety-seven orphaned "babies at the breast." The members located wet nurses, and in some instances, women who had lost children in the epidemic wet-nursed motherless infants. This pairing allowed for adult women and helpless children to offer each other human comfort in a time of sorrow. If no living relative was found for a child, the association arranged for adoption by local citizens.[32]

Orphans of the epidemics of 1847 and 1853 overburdened the means of the Hebrew Benevolent Society and the Ladies' Hebrew Benevolent Society. In 1854, officers of the societies called a meeting and formed the Relief of Jewish Widows and Orphans. Alexander Phillips, Asher Nathan, Edward Shiff and other prominent Jewish businessmen and religious leaders supported the endeavor. The agency built the Jewish Widows and Orphans Home. It was the first organization of its kind in the United States. By 1857, the orphanage housed seventeen children, two infants, and three widows.[33]

In 1852, businessman and philanthropist Judah Touro established the spacious Touro Infirmary as a private and charity hospital in association with Hebrew Benevolent Association. A year later, the infirmary cared for 523 fever cases, 40 percent perished. This high mortality for charitable hospitals was common because the sick did not often arrive until they were in desperate straits. Long after the epidemic, Touro continued to serve the city's poor as part of Tulane University's medical school. [34]

The reports from aid associations and committees from other states indicate that the people of Louisiana empathized with other communities struggling with yellow fever. In 1853, with New Orleans still prostrate from the impact the worst attack of yellow fever in the city's history, the Howard Association mustered the energy to send physicians and aid to Baton Rouge, Thibodaux, and towns in Texas and Alabama. Two years later, despite another significant outbreak of yellow fever in their hometown, more than fifty doctors and nurses from New Orleans embarked on trains to battle the fever in Virginia. Eramus Darwin Fenner, Warren Stone, Thomas Penniston, J.S. McFarlane, Cornelius Beard, and William P. Williams were among the relief delegation. The Norfolk Howard Association awarded the six aforementioned physicians with specially minted gold medals. The decoration included the words "Faith, Hope and Charity" and "Good Samaritan." In acknowledging his award, Williams recalled when he had contracted the disease. He also "felt that philanthropy demanded assistance from . . . the profession in southern cities, where this terrible disease so often prevails; where doctors have opportunities, not, elsewhere afforded, of becoming familiar with its character and the best manner of treating it."[35]

In September, Fenner authored a brief report on the Howard Association hospital in Norfolk before he returned to New Orleans.

Both Fenner and Beard had been involved in the establishment of a temporary hospital in the central section of Norfolk "for the reception of all classes as could not be properly attended in their homes." After departing Norfolk, Fenner rested in Raleigh before returning home. He gleaned the newspapers to monitor the success of his colleagues battling the fever. He also corresponded with Dr. St. Julian Ravenel of Charleston, who remained in Virginia. Fenner mourned the death of three doctors and confided to Ravenel "I learned that my son was

In the 1850s Jewish philanthropist Judah Touro, along with other benefactors of the Hebrew Benevolent Society, established the Touro Infirmary, which treated many yellow fever victims. Image courtesy of the Touro Infirmary Archives, New Orleans, LA.

convalescent from Yellow Fever. I am beginning to be quite uneasy about him."[36]

The only volunteer female nurse who received a medal from Norfolk's Howard Association in 1857 was Annie M. Andrews from southern Louisiana. While summering in Syracuse, she ignored the pleading of family members and left the comfort of upstate New York to help the sufferers. Andrews was one of five civilians singled out for her "philanthropic and invaluable services." In responding to the receipt of the medal, Andrews predicted that "I shall ever hold it a cherished memorial, a bond of union betwixt you and me . . . when, through Providence, I was permitted to cast my mite [*sic*] of sympathy and aid into the rich treasure of kindly care and concern so lavishly poured out for Norfolk in her time of need." Praises for her contribution did not stop with the Norfolk Howard Association. The front-page story of *Harper's Weekly* compared the exploits of Andrews to Florence Nightingale. The weekly noted that she comforted the sick from all walks of life, night and day, and even helped prepare corpses for burial.[37]

Families of yellow fever victims were fortunate if they could secure the remains of their loved one for burial in a family tomb, as shown in the top illustration; many victims' remains simply ended up in mass graves such as the "Yellow Fever Mound" in the Girod Street Cemetery, shown in the bottom photograph as it appeared a decade before removal of the cemetery in 1957.

Chapter Four

YELLOW FEVER IN THE CIVIL WAR ERA

Yellow Jack will grab them up
And take them all away. *

Yellow fever epidemics struck swiftly and swept away hundreds of lives in a season. Americans, however, quickly responded and lent effective assistance. Northern newspapers listed the sizable contributions raised for yellow fever relief. Many of the columns reflected both a sense of civic pride and wishful thinking. There was satisfaction in helping fellow Americans and hope that the contributions might not only help the fever-stricken Southerners get back on their feet, but also mend sectional differences. Even a staunch antislavery newspaper such as the *Liberator* crowed "does not the history of the fever at Norfolk, New Orleans and Savannah prove that the North has a big generous heart, and never fails to respond to the sorrows of the South?"[1]

Southern medical leaders were aware of the region's climatic uniqueness and its associated deadly ailments. Nevertheless, many Southern-born physicians received their training outside of Dixie. With the rise of sectionalism, medical leaders strongly promoted the concept of an education in the South to address regional medical concerns and provide students an education in a Southern environment. The concept that a disease required varying treatment and exhibited different symptoms depending on the country or region where the disease appeared was not unique to the Southern medicine. What was distinct was the passion and ardor in which Southern physicians preached this message. While Southern states did make immediate strides, the subsequent Civil War and Reconstruction had negative repercussions on the growth of medical education in Louisiana and throughout the region. Noted medical historian John Duffy concluded "The exact impact is difficult to measure, but

* As quoted in Gordon Gillson, "The Louisiana State Board of Health: The Formative Years" (Ph.D. dissertation, Louisiana State University, 1960), 177.

there can be little doubt that Southern medicine and Southern medical education suffered a setback of almost half a century." This regression hurt the state's ability to study, combat, and predict epidemics in the latter half of the nineteenth century.[2]

The wistful rhetoric that yellow fever aid was an indication of a united people did not prevent the Civil War. Louisiana was one of the first states to leave the Union and join the new Southern Confederacy. In 1861, the conflict opened with the bombardment of Union-held Ft. Sumter by Confederate artillerists in Charleston, South Carolina under General Beauregard. A year later, federal forces captured New Orleans when the federal fleet under Flag Officer David G. Farragut smashed through the defenses below the city and positioned the fleet along the levees. Fatefully, Farragut had lived in New Orleans in his youth and in 1807, yellow fever took the life of his mother. Naval officer David Porter made the young Farragut his ward and introduced the boy to life in the navy. Completing the circle, Farragut also contracted the fever early in his long naval career.[3]

Similarly, Maj. Gen. Benjamin Franklin Butler, the Union officer who took control of New Orleans, had his own familiar fever tragedy. According to Butler's autobiography, during the War of 1812, the

general's father, John Butler, skippered a privateer and delivered messages to Gen. Andrew Jackson in New Orleans. Butler's brother was named in honor of Old Hickory. Later, John Butler and a portion of his crew died of yellow fever in the British West Indies. Butler recalled "This pestilence and its terrible results was among the first diseases of which I remember ever to have learned from my suffering mother."[4]

Union Army Gen. Benjamin F. Butler's initiation of widespread sanitation measures in New Orleans was met with taunts and ridicule from local residents.

The general quickly evoked orders calling for a firm quarantine and sweeping sanitation policies in the Department of the Gulf. Butler directed an infantry colonel to the forts below New Orleans on the Mississippi River to "establish a strict quarantine at this station, [and] allow no vessel pass (save ships of war of the United States) until the strictest surgical examination, and clean bill of health." Vessels that attempted to ignore the inspection were to be fired upon by the batteries.[5]

Accompanied by his wife and military escorts, Butler examined the city's canal basin. He recounted "the air seemed filled with the most noxious and offensive stenches possible,—so noxious as almost to take away the power of breathing. The whole surface of the canal and the pond was covered with a thick growth of green vegetable scum, variegated with dead cats and dogs or the remains of mules on the banking." Butler directed prisoners and the unemployed to clean the city's public areas. Private citizens assumed responsibility for cleaning their own residences, removing refuse, and whitewashing outside walls with a "solution of lime alum, and salt." Those who refused the cleaning directive faced confinement in the jail.[6]

Despite Butler's sanitary campaign, his officers and soldiers remained skittish about the pending sickly season. White natives prayed that the fever would deliver the city from Union hands and newspapers openly discussed the impact it would have on the soldiers. Confederate sympathizer Julia LeGrand bemused in her journal: "The Yankees have established strict quarantine. The people of the town are frightening them terribly with tales about the yellow fever. We are compelled to laugh at the frequent amusing accounts we hear of the way in which they are treated by boys, Irish women, and the lower classes generally." One of the taunts mocked:

> Yellow Jack will grab them up
> And take them all away.[7]

In personifying the disease, diarist Clara Solomon anticipated that yellow jack's "Appetite will be whetted by abstinence, & how many subjects will be fixed upon. Why N.O. won't be large enough to bury them. The times justify profanity. Already some have died from effects of the sun! How can they stand it in the days to come!" Not knowing the deadly implications, Solomon even confided in her diary that she did not want to be polluted with yankee blood via the mosquitoes and if she killed fewer of the insects, more would live to torment the federals.[8]

This mode of psychological and potential biological warfare by die-hard Confederates was a powerful weapon in undermining federal authority. As the summer approached, the soldiers concocted every possible excuse to leave or get a pass out of the city. Butler was aware of the ruse and thwarted their efforts to depart. According to Butler, none of the army surgeons had experience in combating yellow fever and efforts to enlist the experienced local physicians were unsuccessful.[9]

To provide advice to federal medical personnel, in July 1862, Surgeon Thomas Hewson Bache issued a twenty-page pamphlet titled, *Some Practical Observations on Yellow Fever, Published for the Use of Surgeons of the Volunteer Forces in the Department of the Gulf.* The pamphlet had a cautiously optimistic tone. Bache stressed that while not a single case of fever had been reported that year, "still it is wise and prudent to prepare to counteract evils before they occur." Bache even tried to convince his fellow surgeons that without the fever, New Orleans was a very healthy city. At the same time he advocated the practice of bleeding to reduce pain and the administration of quinine, even though many New Orleans practitioners had "been shaken" by the use of sulphate of quinia.[10]

The fratricidal war notwithstanding, physicians of New Orleans managed to command the respect of their foe and confirm the understanding in medicine at that time of the regional differences in ailments that were generated by a variety of factors. Surgeon Bache showed no reservations about drawing upon the published experiences of the city's healers found in Louisiana medical journals, even though most of those doctors supported the Confederate cause. That Bache cited these doctors as authorities in the midst of the war demonstrated the strength of their reputations. The famous spirit of humanity from New Orleans also radiated during the war. In the autumn of 1862, Confederate Gen. P.G.T. Beauregard dispatched surgeons from his command in Charleston, South Carolina to the fever-racked city of Wilmington, North Carolina. Among the rescuers was the well-respected Dr. Stanford E. Chaillé of New Orleans.[11]

The American Civil War strangled the immigrant influx into New Orleans. The conflict, however, introduced a fresh group of unacclimated arrivals. Federal soldiers from Northern states occupied the city and braced themselves for the fever. Southern coastal cities and marshlands had the reputation for being literally death traps for the unacclimated and New Orleans was at the epicenter of this wave of fear. Patent medicine companies exploited this dismay among the soldiers and their family members. The advertising pages of *Harper's Weekly* of New York City were peppered with notices for curatives, preventives, rejuvenators, and netting aimed at the fears of the soldiers and sailors heading South.

Hostetter's celebrated stomach bitters claimed to be a "positive protective against the fatal maladies of the Southern swamps, and the poisonous tendency of the impure water of Southern rivers and bayous." The Pittsburgh-produced bitters also reportedly saved "unacclimated individuals from epidemic fever," other diseases, and ailments. Made from St. Croix rum, calisaya bark, roots, and herbs, Drake's Plantation bitters supposedly prevented "miasmatic and intermittent fevers." The notice for Holloway's pills and ointment encouraged mothers, wives, and sisters to tuck a few boxes of the aforementioned medication into their loved one's knapsack. The advertisement "insured health even under the exposes of a soldier's life." Another more practical safeguard for the volunteer heading south was mosquito netting. Advertisements for "Musquito Shield or Guard," manufactured by Haven & Co. of New York, en-

HOSTETTER'S

CELEBRATED

STOMACH BITTERS.

☞ **Health of the Army.**—Sickness destroys more soldiers than cannon, rifles, and bayonets. Our brave boys are now suffering more severely from the terrible epidemics which rage in the spring and summer throughout the South, than from the assaults of the public enemy. Is the Government aware that HOSTETTER'S STOMACH BITTERS, the purest stimulant, stomachic, and corrective in existence, is a positive protective against the fatal maladies of the Southern swamps, and the poisonous tendency of the impure water of the Southern rivers and bayous. The Surgeon-General, and the Medical Staff of the Army, are invited, for the sake of the lives of thousands of brave men now fighting for the old flag in infected districts, to give this powerful medicated stimulant a fair trial. Vast quantities of the ordinary alcoholic liquor—all adulterated, all charged with acrid and destructive elements—are used for hospital purposes, in the camp, in the city lazarettos, and in the field. Their effect is murderous; and it is amazing that they should be resorted to, when it is well known to the million, to multitudes of officers and soldiers, and to physicians in civil life, that the use of HOSTETTER'S STOMACH BITTERS will save unacclimated individuals from epidemic fever, dysentery, diarrhœa, liver attacks, fever and ague, and all other complaints specially incident to unhealthy regions, at this perilous season. In the name of common humanity, let this matter be looked to, and that speedily.

Hostetter's Stomach Bitters,

PREPARED AND SOLD BY
    HOSTETTER & SMITH, PITTSBURGH, PA.
DEPOT FOR NEW YORK, 428 BROADWAY.

couraged troops to add netting to the haversack. Cinched with string or elastic, the whalebone-framed bars protected service members and travelers from "musquitoes, flies, or dust."[12]

In Washington, there was also concern about the health of sailors and soldiers as the United States regained control over more and more of the Confederacy. To maintain the navy's effectiveness, in April 1862 Secretary of the Navy Gideon Welles directed that with the "approach of the sickly season upon the Southern coast . . . it [is] imperative that every precaution should be used by the officers commanding vessels to continue the excellent sanitary condition of their crews. The large number of persons known as contrabands flocking to the protection of the United States flag affords an opportunity to provide in every department of a ship, especially boat crews, acclimated labor." Following the secretary's directive, naval officers did enlist blacks in large numbers for the remainder of the war.[13]

On May 12, President Lincoln raised the blockade that allowed trade to return to New Orleans. Secretary of the Treasury Salmon P. Chase then dispatched George S. Denison to ready the customhouse for operations to generate revenue for the federal government by taxing trade goods. Dension was a Vermont-born lawyer who lived and traveled in the South. The flow of revenue was critical to the war effort, so Denison kept his senior informed about his progress and the factors that might hinder his efforts. One of those factors was the threat of fever. In the spring, before Denison left Washington for New

Orleans, he remarked that the "The Southern climate (near the Gulf) is far less healthy for armies than the Northern, but undoubtedly the Federal armies will suffer from sickness no more and probably less, than Southern armies under the same circumstances."[14]

Once in the city, Denison's commentary narrowed to New Orleans. In late June, Denison noted "The city is very healthy and there is no indication as yet, of an epidemic this year." In mid-July, he reported that "The City never was more healthy, and as yet there is no danger of the Yellow Fever." And by late August, a relieved Denison relayed to Chase that "The City is quite healthy and there is no longer much danger from Yellow Fever."[15]

Meanwhile, Butler clashed with consulates during his tenure as military head of the Union forces in New Orleans, because the consulates continued their respective nation's financial relationships with the Confederacy. Butler often caught wind of these "under the table" transactions and reacted with a heavy hand. The apparent uneven enforcement of the quarantine regulations was one of the many bones of contention.[16]

The differences with foreign officials over the quarantine erupted into a duel of words between Butler and the Spanish government. When the American general offered provisions to the Spanish warship *Blasco De Garay* while the ship's supply vessel was quarantined, the Spanish naval commander considered Butler's actions kind, but inconsistent. According to the Spanish, Butler had opened official Spanish correspondence, failed to answer official communications, threatened to expel Spanish officials, and desired to block the arrival of ships coming from Cuba. In contrast, American vessels were not detained in the same manner as the Spanish craft. Butler responded to the accusations by noting that quarantine stations may have detained Spanish vessels longer because ports such as Havana were often infected with yellow fever. Furthermore, Butler desired "to save the inhabitants of New Orleans, as well Spanish as others, from that deadly scourge."[17]

The Spanish consulate countered Butler's measures by not providing craft such as the American schooner *Anna Clapp* with the needed documents to trade in Cuba. The master of the *Clapp* readied to sail from New Orleans to Havana with a mixed cargo, twelve passengers, and a crew of six hands. Yet the consulate Juan Callejon certified "that although this harbor, city [New Orleans] and environs are preserved from other infected ports, considering the bad state of health in this country it is not possible to give a clean bill of health."[18]

In the annual report for 1861, the Louisiana State Board of Health proclaimed that for the first time in more than fifty years there was not a single death recorded from the fever in the city. Yellow fever had appeared in Louisiana but it was confined to isolated cases of mariners delayed at the quarantine station. Butler's directive adhered to the old standard forty-day waiting period for those vessels thought to be a threat with the fever. In reality the quarantine officers regularly shortened this time span. Under martial law, this standard could be maintained but it would have devastated trade in a bustling peacetime economy. In 1862, two cases were reported, but the wartime pattern of only a handful of cases continued until the end of the conflict.[19]

Yellow jack may have been laid low, but so had trade. William Corsan, a British businessmen, lamented "New Orleans, in October 1862, exceeded in dulness [*sic*] any little country-town I ever saw the day after market-day." In peacetime, the fall was the height of the trading season, and a continuation of sluggish financial conditions and rigid quarantine regulations would be a disaster for an international port city.[20]

Outside of the metropolis, Confederate Gen. Mansfield Lovell heard the false rumors that the fever had hit New Orleans. Lovell planned to pin the federals in the city with a large contingent of about 5,500 partisan rangers and as the summer waxed, the fever would take its deadly toll of the vulnerable Yankees. In a dispatch to Beauregard, Lovell concluded "in my judgment the most energetic steps should be taken to confine the enemy to New Orleans, where he must suffer more from sickness than in the country adjoining."[21]

Lovell's strategy failed. The "cleansing" epidemic that the Confederates expected to free New Orleans from Yankee occupation never arrived. Beauregard might have paused upon hearing the plan considering the disease had killed his sister. Diarist Sarah Morgan recorded that rumors circulated that Butler planned to "lay it [New Orleans] in ashes if he is forced to evacuate it from yellow fever or other causes." Regardless of this strategy, Confederates could not hold the federals within the city.

Union soldiers began unauthorized, foraging raids into the surrounding areas and in August 1862, federal forces captured Baton Rouge.[22]

A few Confederates were not content to let "yellow jack" take his own course to eliminate the Northern threat. In the fall of 1862, R.R. Barrow of Terrebonne Parish wrote a lengthy letter to Col. D.F. Fenner outlining Barrow's opinion on the state of affairs. Barrow closed his essay with a plan to carry the yellow plague to the New Orleans. This scheme was similar to the colonial plot by British army officers to spread smallpox among Native Americans with infected blankets and other sundry items. Ninety-nine years later, Barrow postulated:

> I have been surprised that nothing has been done to carry the Yellow fever into N.O. It could be done so easily by sending a man that had already had the disease to some yellow fever Town & there procure fever corpse wrap the dead body in blankets & put them in a metallic coffin. Bring the corpse over & then smuggle the blankets into N.O. Thus started the fever would soon become an epidemic throughout the city. As long as the yankees hold N.O. there will be no yellow fever, for they enforce the quarantine in N.O. It does not in my opinion originate in that place nor in any one of the Old United States.[23]

Inside the city, Butler asserted his authority over civilians and foreign nationals, at times to the chagrin of Lincoln's cabinet members. Furthermore, although he may not have personally gained material wealth during his administrations over Southern cities, some of his associates did prosper. On the other hand, he fed hungry citizens, elevated the status of blacks, and protected his troops from the ravages of fever. His approaches to preventing yellow fever were based on the progressive medical thinking of his time. Butler's two-pronged attack was designed to check the importation of fever from spoiled cargoes or ailing crews and eliminate the spontaneous generation breeding grounds of the fever in the alleys, fetid lots, and industrial areas. At the close of 1862, Lincoln removed controversial Butler from his command in New Orleans. So powerful was the fear of yellow fever that it was not until after the war that a postwar study revealed that the morality rate under Butler's reign remained high despite his sanitation measures.

Gen. Nathaniel P. Banks, Butler's successor, was more concerned with military victories than with sanitation campaigns. Still, ordinances remained in force that required garbage to be placed in collection boxes and other byproducts and large dead animals had to be cleared in twenty-four hours. Hogs were not allowed in the highly populated first and second districts and manure could not be used to fill lots. Military governor Michael Hahn proclaimed on April 6, 1863, that effective May 1, the city was quarantined from the usual Caribbean and Gulf ports. Quarantine changed from forty to ten days, but with the great decline in foreign trade, the incidence of fever subsided during the war. If trade was once again to climb to the antebellum level after the war, risking return of yellow jack would again have to be undertaken.[24]

Following the Civil War, the yellow death reappeared in 1867 and carried away more than 3,100 victims. The vitriolic arguments involving causes and prevention of the fever resumed. The Louisiana sanitarians, part of a national movement, were quick to claim that cleanliness freed cities from the deadly grip of "filth-diseases" during Butler's tenure. Countering this argument, individuals retorted that the fever appeared in the Garden District, one of the cleanest sections of the city. A commerce reporter later proclaimed that this "writer went through all of the worst epidemics in New Orleans, nursed numbers of cases, had the fever and a relapse in a bed in which seven others had laid consecutively, yet in the succeeding epidemic there were no cases in that room. . . . Great stress is laid upon fumigation and cleanliness. It is a well known fact that the fever broke out in the Garden district of New Orleans in 1867, the cleanest and most deodorized and fumigated part of the city, while the dirtiest and most densely populated portions escaped nearly altogether." Importation advocates pointed to the rise in trade and the degeneration of quarantine standards as the reason for yellow jack's return. Indicative of this debate, surgeons in the U.S. government's official Civil War medical history hedged on the issue of local origins or importation of the fever. According to the history, New Orleans remained free of the fever because of both "the institution of active measures of local sanitation and the strict enforcement of quarantine regulations."[25]

From 1862 to 1877, Union soldiers occupied portions of Louisiana. This turbulent period of military occupation, called Reconstruction, often pitted federal authorities, African Americans, resettled Northerners, white Republicans, and former Confederates in a power struggle. Yellow fever played a role in the deployment of troops, the efforts to hold free elections, and racial violence. Before the autumn elections of 1867, Gen. Charles Griffin of the District of Texas was appointed the new head of the larger Fifth District. Fatefully, when yellow fever overwhelmed Galveston the general refused to leave his post and died of the scourge before he assumed command in Louisiana.

In New Orleans, regimental commander John A. Mower became the senior officer in time to see his troops succumb to the fever. Mower sought more troops and the delay of the election because of the raging epidemic. Gen. Philip S. Sheridan, commander of the federal troops in Louisiana, obtained permission from Washington to hire nurses. The fever's fury slackened in the fall, but not before 2,894 civilians and 213 soldiers died. The emergency measures were no longer needed for what the U.S. Army considered a crisis and the locals called a stir. This strain of the virus even killed black soldiers in relatively large numbers, but as expected, the death rate among white soldiers was three and a half times higher than the rate for African American troops.[26]

As the federal soldiers left the city during the epidemic of 1867, Father Peter Leonard Thevis recalled the odyssey of St. Roch from his home in Montpelier, France. Saint Roch nursed victims of the black plague in the 1300s and after his death, believers claimed that Roch's legacy produced miracles. Father Thevis vowed that if none of his parishioners died of the fever that he would construct a church in St. Roch's honor. Remarkably no one from priest's fold perished and keeping his word to God, he led the drive to dedicate a cemetery and construct a mortuary chapel in memory of St. Roch's blessing to the people of New Orleans. Long after the last Louisianians died of the fever, the chapel has become a sanctuary for hopeful victims with a host of ailments. Today, those believers that claimed to be healed by the spirit of St. Roch return with symbolic "ex-votos" that in various ways testify to the miraculous healing process.[27]

The caption of this postcard of St. Roch Chapel in New Orleans reads:

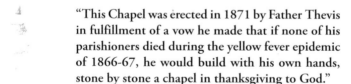

"This Chapel was erected in 1871 by Father Thevis in fulfillment of a vow he made that if none of his parishioners died during the yellow fever epidemic of 1866-67, he would build with his own hands, stone by stone a chapel in thanksgiving to God."

Chapter Five

DEATH WORE A YELLOW ROBE:
THE EPIDEMICS OF THE 1870s

*So many years of happiness
rolled by until the scythe of Time
was sharpened by the plague.* *

After the war, many former Confederates were disgruntled and disenfranchised. They formed political groups such as the White League that terrorized Republican Party office holders and African Americans. The intimidating violence was possible in part because during the summer months, generals William H. Emory and Christopher C. Augur relocated many companies to healthier locales such as Holly Springs in northern Mississippi. In addition, the generals intentionally planned meetings in Washington and vacations in New York during the summer. And the generals directed family members away from Louisiana in the sunny season. The fate of General Griffin may have influenced the officers' travel timetable. In 1870 and 1873, there were two serious outbreaks of fever. When the scourge loomed, commanders and surgeons declared "the prompt removal of troops from points threatened with infection has lessened the ravages of yellow fever at our Southern military stations."[1]

Following the civil conflict, physicians of New Orleans renewed their studies of yellow fever. In 1870, Chaillé completed an insightful work concerning mortality statistics during the war. He demonstrated that there were more deaths caused by disease during the war than in the few years proceeding and following the conflict. He did not determine the cause but he observed that there were both civilians and soldiers living in the city during the summer months who may have been susceptible to other ailments, such as diarrhea (possibly scurvy), malaria, smallpox, and consumption (tuberculosis). The result of Chaillé's study was in direct

* "In Memory of General J.B. Hood," *Southern Historical Society Papers* 32 (1904): 15.

contrast to the assumptions that Butler's sanitation campaign had freed the city of disease by eliminating the filth in selected wards. However, there were no major fever outbreaks in this window of time. Chaillé's statistical analysis was a forerunner of the kind of study conducted by U.S. Army Maj. William Crawford Gorgas in Havana thirty years later. Gorgas's research showed that a strict sanitation campaign reduced the overall mortality statistics in Havana but that the number of yellow fever deaths rose. These results convinced the major that mosquitoes, not poor sanitation, were tied to yellow fever.[2]

Throughout the century, medical leaders from New Orleans continued to shine. Continuing his research in the 1870s, Chaillé, who answered the call for help in Wilmington during the war, headed a yellow fever study commission to Cuba. Chaillé did not discover the source of the fever but made a thorough study of the blood of yellow fever victims searching for a microbial cause, as opposed to a gaseous poison. Medical student Rudolph Matas, a multi-lingual student of great promise accompanied the group as a clerk. In the aftermath of the horrific epidemic of 1878, Congress funded a commission to investigate the origins and causes of yellow fever and other diseases. The advisory Board of Experts included Chaillé, Samuel M. Bemiss, and Col. T.S. Hardee, all of New Orleans.[3]

The germ theory that developed by Europeans slowly gained acceptance in the United States. The theory advanced the idea that a specific type of microorganism is solely responsible for a specific disease. Several causes contributed to the reluctance to accept this position. American scientists lacked high-quality instruments. Laws restricted the experimentation on human patients, although doctors did experiment on charity cases. Many doctors were poorly trained and the hodgepodge of dubious medical schools harmed the profession on the whole. In addition, the American belief in the lethal nature of fomites was not rigorously tested like the germ theory. Not until the 1880s did American physicians embrace the germ theory.[4]

The Reconstruction era presented new challenges and opportunities for the mercantile leaders of New Orleans. Trade had to be revived and railroads had come of age in Louisiana. In addition, new commodities and rival cities looked to steal business away from the Crescent

City. Yellow fever, however, remained a constant. After the war, Edward King, a journalist for *Scribner's Monthly*, visited New Orleans as part of a series of articles on the American South. Of the river port he declared "The bugbear of yellow fever has, for many years, been a drawback to the prosperity of New Orleans. The stories told of its fearful ravages during some of its visitations are startling; but there is hope that the complete and thorough draining of the city will prevent consequent panics in the future."[5]

Even the threat of an epidemic could be expensive. In the late nineteenth century, shipping and commercial newspapers and magazines published all manner of information related to yellow fever and trade. European quarantine notices were issued at the slightest suggestion of an outbreak. In 1874, amidst rumors of the scourge, the editors of the *Nautical Gazette* issued the briefest of notices, "The yellow fever scare is up again." For American mariners and shippers this seven-word message hinted of a long list of hardships, such as time and financial losses, and even death. Certain ports or goods had to be avoided or extra time might be spent at the quarantine station. There was also the expense of fumigation, which could damage the cargo. All of these problems were indirectly communicated with this single-sentence warning.[6]

The *Gazette* followed their terse notice with a confusing article that attempted to unravel the source of some of the rumors that the "plague had made its appearance at several prominent ports." According to the *Gazette*, reporters interpreted a circular reportedly issued by the U.S. secretary of the treasury on how to guard against the fever as tantamount to an announcement of the fever's presence. Evidently, yellow jack did appear in Pensacola, but this was an isolated incident. Dr. Charles B. White, president of the New Orleans Board of Health, flatly denied the fever was in the city. Six days after the appearance of the first notice, the secretary of the treasury issued a second statement that claimed he did not authorize the first circular. The secretary acknowledged that it was his responsibility to generate trade for the benefit of both the commercial interests and the government. In addition, the supervising surgeon who wrote the first notice had not mentioned yellow fever per se, only the sanitary conditions of certain ports.[7]

Several points of interest arise from this discussion. White's claim was correct; in 1874, yellow fever was not a threat in New Orleans. Was there, however, the potential for a conflict of interest to have the secretary of the treasury in charge of marine hospital service because so much of the federal government's revenue was generated from import and export duties? In other words, what was more important to the government: the health of seaman, or generating revenue? Also, the first brief mention of a yellow fever scare in the *Gazette* appeared before the publication of the first circular, so the first circular was not the source for all of the rumors. Debates over the scare in 1874 were commonplace and they reveal the interplay among the press, business factors, city and public health interests, and the state and federal governments.[8]

Community-minded authorities in New Orleans attempted to build upon the foundation of General Butler's sanitation campaigns. Simultaneously, many former Confederates opposed the program simply because of its association with the despised Union general. Progressives assumed that policing the gory meat processing industry would help to check yellow fever and cholera. Butchers and former rebels formed an interesting alliance to oppose legislation to centralize the slaughterhouses in a government-owned yard on the west bank of the Mississippi River. Annually, butchers slaughtered more than 300,000 animals within the city. Entrails, blood, dung, and urine, along with a terrified public, were the byproducts of this operation. Despite these political obstacles, advocates of sanitation continued to implement new means of cleansing the city.[9]

The frightening epidemics the early 1870s prompted the federal government to take a more active role in regulating commerce and public health. State and national politicos saw yellow fever as more than a regional problem. They struggled, however, with the legal issues of authority, the true origins of the fever, and the best balance between commerce and public welfare. Congress formed committees on epidemic diseases to investigate the causes and proper controls for yellow fever. In the spring of 1878, Congress did pass a national quarantine law, but it proved to be weak and generated bad feelings with state governments.[10]

Fixated with the idea that steam, chemical cleansing, or gas could destroy the yellow fever "poison," public health advocates such as

White developed a system for purifying a city. In 1876, he presented his misguided methods to the membership of the American Public Health Association meeting in Boston. Under White's plan, once a case of yellow fever had been pinpointed, sanitation workers deployed in the house of the patient and the entire neighborhood. Using solutions of carbolic

In the 1870s, sanitationists and urban reformers advocated cleaner cities as a method of eliminating epidemics such as cholera and yellow fever. It was thought in this way "His Imperial Agony King Cholera" and yellow jack could be kept in check by a good scrubbing, a fresh coat of white wash, and liberally sprinkling chloride of lime. Image courtesy of the Mariners' Museum Library and Archives, Newport News, VA.

acid, crews sprayed streets and walkways "at a distance supposed to be entirely beyond the presence of the yellow fever poison." Clothing was boiled. In his paper to the association, White reported how repeatedly this procedure immediately curtailed the outbreak of the fever in the infected area.[11]

The New Orleans Board of Health did institute a disinfection program as a means of protecting the city. The policy demanded the cleansing of residences, streets, drains, gutters, and back alleys of sectors thought to be fever-infested. Sulfurous acid gas and carbolic acid were the weapons of choice. The 70 percent mixture of carbolic acid included chloride of iron and zinc extracted from scrap tin cans. Carbolic acid, or phenol, had been used in the United Kingdom as a disinfectant to protect public health and in the operating rooms of Dr. Joseph Lister. It was Lister's groundbreaking method of cleansing the air during surgery that saved the lives of countless patients from infection. However, the acid had little impact on the flying insects. On the other hand, the five pounds of sulfur burned to purify an average room was harmful to mosquitoes if it was applied effectively.[12]

During the outbreak of 1873, Dr. Alfred W. Perry, sanitary inspector for the board of health, made extensive use of carbolic acid. Workers with hand-sprinkling pots and three-man teams directing hoses from water carts distributed the solution. Laborers applied the acid as fast as a horse walked. About seventy gallons of acid were used per block. The acid was aimed at a yellow fever germ. The term "germ" was used in a general sense. Nevertheless, this was a departure from previous thinking about a miasmic cloud. In the fourth district, "thirty entire squares and twenty-one half squares where yellow fever had occurred were thus disinfected." In seven of these cleansed areas the fever reemerged. This low reoccurrence level was thought to be proof of the effectiveness of the procedure. Occasionally, the process was repeated.[13]

In 1878, the carbolic disinfection process was again implemented, but with poor results. The solution was then five to ten parts water to one part acid. After August 14, official switched the emphasis to burning sulfur. Despite claims to the contrary, this so-called blanket cure irritated eyes and caused headaches and nausea. At the time, it was thought a more pure form of carbolic acid would eliminate these discomforts, but a stronger form of this organic acid would have aggravated these unpleasant side effects.[14]

The Union troops departed in 1877, and former Confederates wrestled control of the government from all contenders. The high-level decision to regularly transfer military units out of Louisiana before summer's arrival foretold of a problem the federal government encountered during the Spanish-American War twenty-one years later. If Americans sought to exert maximum influence in the Caribbean, yellow fever had to be mastered. As for New Orleans in the 1870s, the city was in desperate financial and political straits. Trade remained stagnant. Corruption was commonplace. The State Board of Health was in political turmoil and recovering from the effects of the war. Although there was a growing national effort to curb the spread of diseases, public health issues in the municipality languished amongst the turmoil and drive to restore commerce.[15]

Set during an economic recession, the epidemic of 1878 spread from Louisiana to Mississippi, Arkansas, Missouri, Tennessee, Kentucky, Ohio, New York, New Jersey, Pennsylvania, Illinois, and Indiana. Of the estimated 100,000 to 125,000 cases perhaps as many as 25,000 people died. Railroads and steamboats played a major role in transporting the vector mosquitoes and the contagious victims to uninfected areas and New Orleans was ground zero for this cataclysmic epidemic.[16]

Pres. Rutherford B. Hayes made eloquent appeals to private citizens to support the relief efforts. There was fear that a massive famine would follow the epidemic, and the secretary of war soon exhausted

During the epidemic of 1878, horse-drawn chemical tanks sprinkled carbolic acid on the city streets as a means of killing the "yellow fever germ." This method contributed very little to the suppression of the epidemic.

the resources available for aid. Hayes, in his State of the Union address, bemoaned that the "enjoyment of health by our people generally has, however, been interrupted during the past season by a fatal pestilence (the yellow fever) in some portions of the Southern States, creating an emergency which called for prompt and extraordinary measures of relief."[17]

A steamer may have introduced the disease to New Orleans from Havana in May, but a formal announcement of the fever's arrival in the *Picayune* was not made until the end of July. Even then, the ailment was described strictly as a "strangers' disease." At the same time, the towboat *John Porter* chugged up the Mississippi River towards Pittsburgh. All told, twenty-three people on board perished before the *Porter* ended her deadly journey.[18]

On May 15, Gov. Francis T. Nicholls issued an order requiring detention and fumigation of all incoming vessels. Problems arose immediately concerning implementation of the new ruling. Some fruit importers complained that disinfection with sulfur fumes and carbolic acid ruined their cargoes. Shortly thereafter, Dr. Samuel Choppin, president of the board of health, exempted selected fruit vessels. The board was caught between conflicting public health and short-term commercial interests. In this scenario, the business interests won with tragic results.[19]

To check the fever, beginning in June 1878, Louisiana's board of health placed a virtual embargo on New Orleans' tropical commerce, especially the growing fruit trade to Eastern cities. This segment of trade eventually played an important role in reviving commerce because the city was now connected to Eastern markets through a network of railroads. Lemons from the Mediterranean, bananas from Central America, and coffee from Brazil were exchanged for cotton for European markets. By the 1890s, about twelve million banana bunches were imported. This trade, however, threatened to import fever into the city. In addition to the fruit being from regions endemic to yellow fever, the mosquitoes could consume any sugary residue and juice the fruit exuded.[20]

It was not until August 15 that Choppin unofficially informed the Howards that an epidemic had existed in the city for some days. On August 16, a meeting was called, but membership was low. At the end of the epidemic, there were twenty-two members, eighteen of them new.

In mid-September only a half dozen Howards were well enough to offer their services. Remarkably, none of the ill members died. Fortunately, Howard assistants stationed in the suburbs of Carrollton and across the river in Algiers were able to extend the association's helping hand.[21]

As in the recent past, the board of health sprinkled carbolic acid along infected blocks. Edwin Brittin Jennings, a sales manager for the commission merchants C.H. Lawrence and Company during the dreadful summer of 1878, wryly remarked "my nostrils have feasted on that odor for two months & I can't say I enjoyed it either." He concluded that the trouble, expense, and irritation did little to curb the fever and noted that a friend had every room in his house cleaned with carbolic acid but still "worried himself into having" the fever.[22]

Jennings corresponded with his uncle, Dr. Roscoe Green Jennings in Little Rock, Arkansas, and other members of the family. Jennings's employers had departed for safer environs, leaving their associate to manage a good portion of the business. His letters reveal not only stress during an epidemic, but also explain how information was exchanged during those perilous times. He sent his letters to Little Rock via Cincinnati or St. Louis, perhaps because Arkansas established a quarantine against goods, travelers, and mail that originated in New Orleans. Above all, Jennings confided to his uncle "I sincerely pray it will not be long before we have the frost."[23]

An innocent conversation Jennings had with a reporter from the *Picayune* had unfortunate consequences. The journalist later wrote "A young friend, who has received a letter from an uncle living in Little Rock, Ark., informs us that the yellow fever scare, or panic, has reached that place, though there is not a case of that disease within 135 miles." This was not Jennings's first entanglement with the press. A descriptive note he sent to his uncle had appeared in an Arkansas paper much to his regret. News of the published letter then reached New Orleans. This type of reporting countered the efforts of businessmen to promote the city's image and curb details concerning the horrors of the epidemic.[24]

By August, some Gulf Coast governments, including Mobile, issued a quarantine against New Orleans. The blockade, however, was not universal, as smaller towns hoped to maintain their commercial ties with the Crescent City. Fleeing refugees spread the fever to Mississippi.

In that same month, Surgeon Gen. John M. Woodworth of the Marine Hospital Service issued mortality and morbidity statistics with his weekly reports. In the first week of August, there were almost two hundred new cases and "four principal points of infection, and these spreading; but the board of health hopes to control it." Despite the surgeon general's optimism, the fever fanned out across the Deep South and headed toward Tennessee.[25]

In the Northeast, Midwest, and across the former Confederacy, ethnic, civic, and veterans' organizations raised a collective cry for help. The veterans of the Louisiana Division of the Army of Northern Virginia appealed for aid from other division members. The Louisiana chapter sought to "help its members and its families, who are in need because of this fearful malady." In that same spirit, members of the Société Française de Secours Mutuels de Lafayette of Brooklyn offered donations to the "Yellow Victims in the Southern States," and scores of Northern physicians and nurses ventured South to confront the fever.[26]

In this scene from 1878, young boys in New York City serve as runners to assist transport wagons in the collection of donated goods for victims during the nation's greatest yellow fever epidemic. Image courtesy of the Mariners' Museum Library and Archives, Newport News, VA.

The Young Men's Christian Association in New York and the yellow fever relief committee members organized a massive clothing collection drive. The effort canvassed thirty city blocks. Telegraph boys ran ahead of a procession of thirty company wagons to contact potential donors. In one day, the caravan collected about 4,500 cubic feet of articles, including blankets, bedding, mattresses, and clothing. In the spirit of reconciliation, *Harper's Weekly* exclaimed, the "necessity for help is urgent, to avoid worse calamities. The people of the North do not require entreaty to give freely, and they will not cease to give their Southern brethren in need their sympathy and assistance." Financier John P. Morgan spearheaded the charity effort as treasurer of the Peabody and Citizens Relief Association of New York and Southern Relief Committee of the New York City Chamber of Commerce. City leaders also placed ballot boxes in saloons, restaurants, and post offices to collect donations.[27]

Though not the worst epidemic in the city's history, the epidemic of 1878 was poignant. From a population base of about 211,000, an estimated 40,000 people fled. Of the more than 10,000 cases, approximately 4,050 people died, including about 150 African Americans. The Howard Association assisted 5,132 African American patients, of

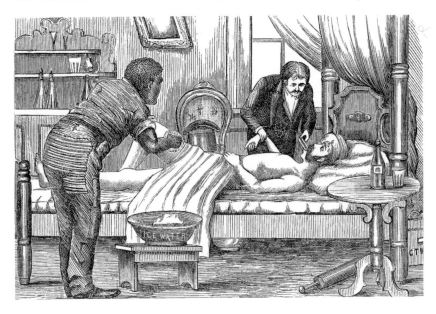

Illustration from *Doctor Dispachemquic*, a satirical treatment of the 1878 New Orleans yellow fever epidemic.

whom only 2.6 percent died. Among the whites who died, more than 2,300 were children under the age of sixteen. This figure included a notably high number of native-born four-year-old males. Established middle-class families who expected immigrants to be the primary victims were horrified when their own young ones perished. Thus, the long-held belief in Creole superiority was shaken.[28]

On a personal level, Elizabeth Caroline Merrick had spent her life with the threat of the fever. After the Merricks moved to New Orleans, they often summered at the springs of Virginia. When Elizabeth Merrick's daughter, Laura, married Louis J. Bright, Merrick continued to encourage her child to depart before the warmer seasons arrived. At the insistence of her husband, however, Laura remained in the city. At the height of the fever's fury, Laura fell victim to the virus. Writing with great anguish more than twenty years later in her memoirs, Merrick cursed the poor judgment of her son-in-law and the loyal and submissive character of her daughter that led Laura to defer to her husband's demands. Drawing from the observations of the attending minister, the mother recorded that Laura exhibited "the calm fortitude she manifested even when she kissed her children good-by, Breathing softly she went to sleep and closed her sweet eyes on the world—forever."[29]

Unlike Elizabeth Merrick, George Washington Cable, a budding novelist and an accountant for the cotton factor and commission merchant Wm. C. Black & Company, did not leave the city when the fever threatened. Two of Cable's brothers-in-law who worked at the same firm did send their respective families to outlying smaller communities, but Cable's family remained in New Orleans. One in-law moved in with Cable's family; the other boarded elsewhere in the city. When the fever struck, the nightmare Cable later described as a "long and gloomy story" unfolded.[30]

The fever victims included four of the writer's children, his wife, brothers-in-laws, his sisters' families, neighbors, a servant, and the servant's child. Cable nursed an ill brother-in-law, but the relative died "a horrible death" leaving Cable's sister and "three little children without a farthing in this world." Cable's second brother-in-law arrived at Cable's house following a family visit in the country. The surviving brother-in-law endured a tremendous ordeal to reach the Cable home, walking and taking a freight train and a cab. He wandered, stumbled, and vomited for about fifteen hours before reaching the Cable's house. Remarkably, the man recovered.[31]

Young George, one of Cable's children, died and the "horrible fetor [*sic*] of yellow fever filled the whole house." Cable's third daughter "a little nervous frail thing," was also stricken, followed by a third child. In Cable's words, all the children "were threatened with black-vomit—a thing which cannot be imagined more loathsome and frightful than it is, it is almost always followed closely by death." Just before nightfall, Cable remembered that his son "dear little George left us for a better world." The parents steathfully buried the youngster in the middle of the night to protect the fragile mental well-being of the surviving siblings. Slowly,

Author George Washington Cable's writings were deeply influenced by his own tragic experiences with yellow fever in New Orleans, including his loss of several family members to the disease.

patients began to recover. Supportive friends, neighbors, and Howard nurses came to care for the Cable sick, giving the couple a much needed rest.[32]

Soon, however, word came of the death of his eldest daughter and the kindly neighbor. In a letter to a colleague, Cable hoped that his friend never had to endure the crying, screaming, and moaning of his own offspring consumed with the fever. Southern literary scholar Louis D. Rubin, Jr. noted that the dark mystique of fever surfaced at least half a dozen times in the novelist's subsequent body of work, and that the "experience left a deep scar on Cable's mind." An example of the fever in Cable's work appeared in *The Grandissimes: A Story of Creole Life.* In the novel, Joseph Frowenfeld, an American newcomer, languished on the edge of life as "the unsated fever was running through every vein and artery, like soldiery through the streets of a burning city, and far down the caverns of the body the poison was ransacking every palpitating corner, the poor immigrant fell into a moment's sleep."[33]

The Howard nurses mentioned in Cable's letter were just one component of the Howard Association. As the group's reputation grew, it became a clearinghouse for supplies, medical personnel, and monetary contributions from outside of the state. In 1878, Claiborne County Mississippi's board of health quarantined the county against the threat of fever from New Orleans. Nurses dispatched by the Howards, however, were allowed to enter the town. Before the end of the summer, the Howards announced they were no longer in need of contributions. The following months revealed this announcement was an honest but extremely regrettable mistake. Lesser-known charities from more than eighty towns in the region began to turn to Howards for financial assistance. The Howards fell into debt and could not answer the call for help.[34]

The press and other charities questioned the judgment and the integrity of the Howards. The Howards had distributed more than eight million dollars to ten organizations and helped to establish the New Orleans Peabody Association, but the demand for support grew. In addition, the U.S. secretary of state queried the Howards about a cash reserve, and, after the epidemic, the newly formed Howards Physicians' Society thought they were underpaid. Through it all, the Howards elected to suffer in silence.[35]

Overreaching efforts to distribute money and supplies efficiently across multiple states and provide leadership to related organizations overwhelmed the Howard volunteers. Furthermore, groups such as the Young Men's Christian Association deferred to the reputation of the Howard Association and only reluctantly joined the relief efforts because of a lack of organization, ability, and name recognition. Nonetheless, the YMCA and associates gathered $81,541.20. The expenditures included stationery, gas, bedding, blankets, rent, food, and stimulants, as well as the services of laborers, cabbies, nurses, physicians, and clerks. With the assistance of the Peabody Association and the New Orleans Relief, they administered to 5,071 registered fever cases (3,714 whites and 1,357 African Americans) but had to turn away an innumerable applicants. The YMCA also distributed more than 100,000 rations.[36]

The late construction of a railroad network linking New Orleans to those Eastern markets and interior trade hubs also offered major avenues for the pestilence to spread from the coast to other cities. In 1854, Gov. Paul O. Hebert of Louisiana predicted that because rail lines tied New Orleans to smaller towns in the state, the city's sanitation problems would soon become a statewide issue. Even though poor sanitation was not the cause of the fever, the governor foresaw how fixed transportation ties would make yellow fever a threat to all of Louisiana. As the governor had projected, in 1867 and 1878, the fever spread quickly across the state and west into Texas, east into Mississippi, and north into Tennessee, in part via rail transportation.[37]

What Hebert had forecast, the general public also grasped. Entire villages could be decimated by fever imported from New Orleans. To check the pale horse of pestilence, local vigilantes armed with shotguns and town leaders compelled sealed trains to speed through their towns without stopping. This grassroots approach to prevention disrupted communication, mail and passenger service, and the delivery and transfer of freight. Furthermore, these quarantines isolated New Orleans from the medical supplies and foodstuffs during outbreaks. The far-flung epidemic of 1878 only fueled the vigilantes' activities and cut off those communities in need of aid.[38]

Railroad executives also understood that if the trains were not permitted to halt and exchange passengers and cargo, services could not be guaranteed. Consequently, in 1878, the Illinois Central Railroad curtailed service to the South. Mail trains halted a mile beyond their scheduled stops to deliver the mail and passengers with the proper health certificates. In Chicago, railroad stock prices fell. The cost estimates for medical expenses, funerals, and trade losses for the 1878 epidemic ranged from just under eleven million to more than fifteen million dollars.

Yellow fever was as much a plague on commerce as people. The caption of the engraving read "The cessation of business—idleness on the levee." As other ports established quarantines against New Orleans in 1878, maritime traffic would not flow from the river port. Many working-class people, such as these African American stevedores, did not have the financial means to leave during an epidemic.

Despite these tremendous losses, the people of New Orleans normally bounced back from these disasters. Yet, when the fever appeared in the following year, even though the outbreak was relatively mild, the collective effects of three epidemics in the same decade, a national economic depression, and the loss of part of the busy trade seasons served to dampen spirits, choke business, and shatter expectations of a swift recovery.[39]

The burgeoning city of Atlanta exploited the tradition of yellow fever in New Orleans, Savannah, and Memphis. Leaders in the Georgia city incorrectly claimed that because of their city's high altitude and clean environment it was protected from yellow fever. In 1878, they built a hospital for 3,000 fever refugees, encouraged their arrival, and enjoyed their best business year to date. Some of the refugees became permanent residents. In the 1880s, Atlanta relished tremendous economic growth due in part to its key geographic location for railroads, forceful entrepreneurs, and the postwar epidemics in other Southern commercial hubs.[40]

Not content to endure continued financial losses, Louisiana businessmen created the Auxiliary Sanitary Association of New Orleans. The association promoted broad strokes of public health reform. It grew from six founders to thousands of contributing subscribers. The epidemic of 1878 cost in "money and trade from $175,000,000 to $200,000,000—as great as the loss from the Chicago fire," according to one contemporary source. That same source suggested that proper sanitary expenses would have cost "one-twentieth of that amount." It was this fresh mindset that sparked businessmen to reshape their views on sanitation.[41]

The appalling national losses fueled the ongoing yellow fever controversies in New Orleans. After the epidemic, a mayor-selected panel reported that 4,000 cartloads of kitchen garbage had been returned to the city to fill potholes. The panel claimed that if this transplanted refuse was not the source of the fever then it served as a catalyst. And once yellow jack took hold "the roll of death added new victims to the feast." Capitalizing on the sanitation and charity issues, John C. Fleming of the Workingman's Party spearheaded a biracial political movement. Fleming clamored that the neglected needs of hundreds of labor-class victims demanded retribution. If the social and public health issues were not enough, reports circulated that when returning refugees reopened their homes, the yellow threat resurfaced because the houses harbored the fever. There was also resistance to exhuming hastily buried bodies for fear of generating another fever outbreak.[42]

As in the past, shipping was linked to yellow jack during the decade after the Civil War. In 1873, a Spanish sailor from Havana was associated with that year's epidemic. Dr. Samuel Choppin declared the source of the fever in 1878 was the steamer *Emily B. Souder* three and a half days out of Havana via Key West. It cleared the Mississippi River Quarantine Station on May 12, with a crew member who was sick and later hospitalized. The engineer and purser also carried the virus but showed no outward symptoms. They came down with the fever after the steamer docked at the foot of Calliope Street in New Orleans. Both men died before the end of the month.[43]

In 1879, Congress created the National Board of Health (NBH), an advisory and investigative agency headed by Dr. John S. Billings, in response to the cry for greater involvement of the national government in overseeing the federal quarantine. Many Southern citizens did not trust the Louisiana officials to be forthcoming with timely and complete information concerning yellow fever and the possible threat of fever. Eventually, the Gulf Coast states and Tennessee signed an agreement that required the earliest possible notification of a yellow fever outbreak.

Representative James A. Garfield was one of the key members of the U.S. House Committee on Yellow Fever. Frustrated with the politics and complexity of the issues, Garfield vented in his diary that "I fear we are in danger of making ourselves ridiculous. It is a question of science to be handled by a town meeting. . . . In getting experts to aid us, our committee seem bent on getting each a special friend appointed." A joint committee received expert reports on the origins of the fever. According to Garfield, only one doctor, however, "held that the disease is not indigenous, but is imported from tropical countries, particularly West India [*sic*] islands." In essence, the experts implied that quarantines would not check the fever.[44]

Despite strong sentiments against the state, Dr. Bemiss of the University of Louisiana (now Tulane University) accepted a position on the NBH's Board of Experts. In addition, there was a growing push for a unified approach to public health. In that same spirit, attendees at the seventh American Public Health meeting of 1879 in Nashville exchanged ideas on the reporting of yellow fever, acclimation, duties of boards of health, isolation of the city and infected cities, and the prevention of the spreading of saffron scourge by railroad trains.[45]

In conjunction with the creation of the NBH, Congress passed a national quarantine act. Quarantine stations were often isolated islands near major trade centers. Health officials inspected the crews, passengers, cargoes, ships, and ballasts for health signs that might endanger the port. Once the vessel was given a clean bill of health, the ship was cleared to proceed. Those vessels that showed signs of poor health, or hailed from infectious ports could be isolated until such time as the local authorities deemed it safe for the vessel to proceed. Violators faced fines and imprisonment. In Louisiana, the state quarantine stations for oceangoing craft were located near the mouth of the Mississippi River.

As early as 1647, the Massachusetts Bay Colony instituted quarantine measures against Barbados to protect against smallpox and yellow fever. In 1799, Congressional legislation placed federal employees involved with quarantine enforcement under the Department of the Treasury, but these employees often played an auxiliary role in supporting state and municipal officials. The act of 1878 required the construction of federal quarantine stations. The federal Gulf Coast facility was built on Ship Island. Starting in 1878, the government issued the *Bulletin of Public Health* for the station operators and public health associates. The following year, the bulletin ceased, but was revised under the new title *Weekly Abstract of Sanitary Reports*. The location of the Ship Island station did not serve trade to New Orleans well, and, once again, Southern politicians objected to the perceived intrusion of their respective state's sovereignty.[46]

To expedite the quarantine process, an official not only isolated and inspected the vessels and their cargoes but also fumigated and disinfected the ships. For yellow fever, these methods had mixed results. The stations, such as Ship Island, served as the outposts for disease detection, and several medical officers contracted the yellow fever while performing their duties. Eventually, custom-fitted vessels were configured with the chemical storage, pumps, and hoses needed to fumigate large ocean-going vessels.[47]

The NBH and the federal quarantine system had a troubled birth. The quarantine efforts survived despite a faulty start. The NBH did not. The NBH faded after four years for a variety of reasons. John S. Billings, head of the NBH, attempted to expand the authority and enlarge the budget of the fledgling organization. Surgeon Gen. John B. Hamilton, head of the Marine Hospital Service, saw the NBH as a threat to the service. Northern business factions were leery of possible additional controls on trade and the fees charged for inspection and fumigation. Southern politicians and state pubic health officers considered the NBH an intrusion and a threat to their authority. Despite popular support, four years later, Congress cut the funding and functions of the NBH.[48]

Spearheading the Southern crusade against the NBH was Dr. Joseph Jones, president of the Louisiana State Board of Health. The outspoken and egotistical Jones was a formidable opponent. A prolific writer and respected educator, he resisted the establishment of the gulf quarantine station because of its infringement on the state's rights. Jones's campaign, however, further strained the relationships between Louisiana and the surroundings states. The Sanitary Council of the Mississippi Valley supported the NBH and distrusted the Louisiana State Board of Health. Closer to home, Jones even crossed swords with the New Orleans Auxiliary Sanitary Commission and the New Orleans Medical and Surgical Association over their support of the NBH. This clash with state associations probably accelerated his retirement to private life. Jones's departure signaled the end of Louisiana's struggle for public health autonomy.[49]

Trying to capitalize on the federal government's new found interest in quarantines and the role the frost played in quelling the fever, Dr. John Gamgee developed the idea of refrigeration ship stations. The massive ships would freeze both ship and cargo. Gamgee claimed "once yellow-fever poison . . . is subjected to a temperature below 32°, it is gone at once and for always." New Orleans would be one of the locations for these floating refrigeration stations. At first blush, the writers for *Scientific American* were supportive, and noted the "experiment would seem to be worthy of a trial, and, properly conducted, would be comparatively inexpensive." Later, however, the inventor's magazine was skeptical. The publication noted "We have no positive proof of the existence of living organisms; still less proof that frost kills them." Gamgee's plan did receive support in Congress but never came to fruition.[50]

With the fever thought to have spread by contact with the dead, local ordinances curtailed exhuming the dead, wakes, and the public viewing of the remains. In 1879, it was reported that returning refugees contracted the fever when they reopened their infected homes where family members had died. It was acknowledged that "Wealthy families, no doubt, find it painful to leave their dead in potters' fields, but personal feeling should not be suffered to endanger the entire community." To accommodate both the secular and ecclesiastical laws, clergy members directed the construction of mortuary chapels in or near cemeteries. This arrangement allowed for complete burial rights and answered the concerns for public safety. One of the first churches of its kind was built in

Built in 1826, the Old Mortuary Chapel (Our Lady of Guadalupe Catholic Church), was intended to remove funural services for yellow fever victims outside the Vieux Carré and closer to city cemeteries.

1826 and became known as the Old Mortuary Chapel. This structure, now called Our Lady of Guadalupe still stands, and is one of the oldest houses of worship in the city.[51]

The outbreak of 1879 was allegedly curtailed by a focused campaign to clean public streets. The effort was credited for limiting much of the fever's impact to the western parishes. Although there was little doubt that the fever originated in New Orleans, the outbreak was noteworthy because of its mildness and that it struck in the affluent districts. Among the city's relatively few victims were former Confederate Gen. John Bell Hood, the general's wife, Anna Marie Hennen Hood of New Orleans, and Lydia, oldest of their eleven children. Surviving many wounds, the general was struck down by an invisible virus that also ravaged the Southland. In the words of Ida Richardson Hood, one of the couple's seven surviving daughters, "So many years of happiness rolled by until the scythe of Time was sharpened by the plague."[52]

Hood's fate epitomized the South's Lost Cause. In battle, Hood was fearless but also reckless as the commander of larger units. He lost both an arm and a leg in service to the Confederacy. After the war, Hood helped to establish a cotton factor and commission merchant firm in New Orleans. Times were difficult for mercers, however, so he switched to the insurance business. Hood spent much of his later life researching

his memoirs that defended his rash military decisions. Following his death, Hood's associates issued his martial autobiography, *Attack and Retreat: Personal Experiences in the United States and Confederate States Armies*. General Beauregard was one of his comrades who assisted in the publication. The book served as a fund-raiser to support the surviving children. A famous photograph of the

Confederate Gen. John Bell Hood

siblings circulated as part of the promotional efforts of the Hood Family Relief Committee.[53]

Hood's death was not the only reminder of the Civil War. On March 3, 1879, the *New York Times* printed a scathing article attacking the leaders of New Orleans and Memphis for their failure to take definitive action against the fever. The paper reported that the city streets remained filthy and bodies were being exhumed despite the alleged possibility that this activity might revitalize the fever. Furthermore, the piece reported, perhaps because of a mild winter, the fever had already reappeared before spring. Having experienced a horrific epidemic the following summer, the *Times* trumpeted in a tone reminiscent of the days before the Civil War that "If the Southern cities are to permit the infection to survive the Winter, and continue to neglect every precaution against the renewal of its deadly ravages, any effort of the National Government in their behalf would be rendered futile." Clearly, there was mounting pressure on New Orleans to address a deadly problem that might start in the Crescent City but threaten the entire nation.[54]

Hood, his oldest daughter, Ida Richardson, and his wife, Anna Marie Hennen Hood, were all casualties of the relatively small 1879 yellow fever outbreak. General Hood left behind ten orphaned children ranging in age from two months to ten years old; the vacant chair in the lower right represents the death of eleven-year old Lydia.

Chapter Six

STATES RIGHTS AND NATIONAL REFORMS, 1880s-1890s

The term MARITIME SANITATION is of recent origin, and signifies the application of modern methods suggested by sanitary science and approved by experience in the treatment of all carriers,persons, and things traversing the seas. *

Following the death of Margaret Gaffney Haughery the citizens of New Orleans went into mourning. Margaret's family had left Ireland and settled in Baltimore. By the age of nine, Margaret was an orphan. Her parents apparently were victims of a yellow fever epidemic. Luckily, Welsh neighbors who had immigrated to America on the same ship as the girl's family adopted the orphan. Later she married Charles Haughery, and the couple moved to New Orleans. She lost her husband and a baby within a year. A tireless worker, Haughery toiled as a laundress, food vendor, and baker. She overcame her illiteracy and established numerous small businesses.[1]

Not forgetting her tragic childhood, Haughery, with help from Sister Regis Barrett of the Sisters of Charity, built St. Theresa's Orphan Asylum for girls. And as her charges and responsibilities grew, so did Haughery's personal wealth and business empire. As a baker, Haughery became known as "The Bread Woman." In 1853, she helped many fever victims, attending to anyone regardless of race or religious background. The epidemic created the need for more care for orphans and subsequently, the Sisters of Charity opened St. Elizabeth's home. Haughery, a devout Catholic, supported four orphanages for children of all faiths.[2]

When Haughery passed away in 1882, the archbishop and governor attended her funeral. Former mayors and governors served as her

---

* John Holt, *An Epitomized Review of the Principles and Practice of Maritime Sanitation* (New Orleans, 1892), 7.

pallbearers. She was buried alongside Sister Regis. Businesses and city offices closed. Her estate was valued at more than $600,000 and most of it was distributed among the orphanages. Two years after her death, she was one of the first women in the United States to have a statue erected in her honor. Resting in the park also named for the great philanthropist, the monument is simply inscribed "Margaret." In that same spirit, in 1888, Louisianans donated almost $7,200 to relieve the suffering in Jacksonville and experienced New Orleans nurses offered their services to the Floridians.[3]

The year Haughery died, Rudolph Matas made two important contributions to conquering Bronze John. He translated an article

Statue of Margaret Gaffney Haughery

penned by Dr. Carlos Juan Finley of Cuba for the *New Orleans Medical and Surgical Journal*. Finley's thesis correctly suggested that the *A. eygpti* mosquito was the vector of yellow fever. Finley's work, however, remained obscure for almost twenty years and was not substantiated until Maj. Walter Reed's commission confirmed the Cuban's findings. Later, Matas traveled to Brownsville to battle yellow fever. One of Matas's patients was William C. Gorgas. Then a captain, Gorgas would later be responsible for vigorously eradicating the breeding environment of mosquitoes in Havana and the Panama Canal Zone.[4]

Also in the 1880s, Joseph Holt and Joseph Jones, New Orleans physicians and educators, emerged as national leaders in public health. Holt and Jones were cast from the same mold. Jones was the son of a prominent Georgia minister/planter. He was educated at Princeton and the present-day University of South Carolina. When he joined the medical department of what is now Tulane University, he brought with him a sizable ego and a considerable knowledge of pubic health, chemistry, medicine, and natural history. Jones campaigned against the sickly image of the South and the encroachment by the federal government on state health controls. He also earned numerous awards and held prestigious offices, including chairman of the Section of Public and International Hygiene at the Ninth International Medical Congress, the presidency of the Louisiana State Medical Society, and an honorary presidency of the Section of Physiology at the first Pan-American Medical Congress.[5]

Under Holt's leadership, a unified system of classification, inspection, isolation, and fumigation processed incoming vessels. Inspectors gave craft a rating from first to fourth class based on the healthiness of the ship, cargo, passengers, crew, and the ship's port of origin. The initial inspection occurred at Port Eads, about one hundred and ten miles from New Orleans. If the vessel received a high rating, it proceeded to an upper quarantine station located seventy miles from the city to be given the complete sanitary treatment and was normally delayed between six hours and five days. If the vessel earned a fourth class rating, officials directed the ship to Lower Station for a thorough cleaning at Pass a L'Outre, a seldom-used passage to the Mississippi River.[6]

The state board of health made a compromise in consideration of the value of the fruit trade versus the fear of fever importation. During the summer and early fall, the board requested that the fruit-laden ships utilize only acclimated crew members. Furthermore, only produce from the plantation could be imported; passengers were not allowed and "the ship and all on board must undergo quarantine the same as required of all other vessels bringing passengers and cargo from intertropical American and West Indian ports." This was an attempt to establish a fragile balance between a year-round, active port and the desire to protect the public.[7]

Ships were cleansed with a solution of about 1,500 gallons of bichloride of mercury. Crew quarters were purified with carbolic fluids or other disinfectants. Hatches were secured and a pipe was run below decks through which sulfurous oxide gas fumigated the sealed hulls. Certain cargoes such as coffee and fruits had to be removed first. Bedding and all manner of textiles including mosquito netting were steam cleaned. A specially fitted tug with a modified commercial laundry chamber, boilers, fumigating furnace, pipes, and fans worked in conjunction with an elevated tank of 8,000 gallons of bichloride of mercury. Teams processed most ships in a few hours. Proud of the system, Holt published and lectured widely on maritime sanitation procedures.[8]

Holt was a firm believer in the germ theory and was convinced that his sanitation system eliminated the deadly microorganism that caused yellow fever. Although the true nature of the disease's dissemination was not yet known, the fumigation method was harmful to mosquitoes. The bichloride of mercury could also harm the insects if it came in contact with them (not to mention that some of the disinfectants were harmful to people). The standardized procedures of fumigation and rigid inspections may explain the decline in fever outbreaks in the city.[9]

Those experts who concluded that microbial agents were the cause of the fever presumed that infectious particles of yellow fever infested the remains of the dead, certain cargoes, mail, and clothing. The disease was transferred when these inanimate carriers were shifted from one location to the next. In 1889, Dr. C.P. Wilkinson, the president of the Louisiana State Board of Health, declared that "it is certain that infection from an infected town is frequently brought in the baggage of passengers, in the effects of the crews, and in the cargo and the confined air of the holds of vessels."[10]

The same public health push to sanitize ships was also applied to trains. The need to improve passenger cars became a regular topic of discussion at the American Public Health Association conventions. The association even formed a committee on car sanitation that included ideas on disinfecting cars, better ventilation, and cleaner drinking water. These measures represented a merger between the old school sanitationists and advocates of germ theory.[11]

Merging public health with business during the epidemic in 1897, the Louisville and Nashville Railroad published numbered circulars of curtailed routes issued as "yellow fever bulletins." As the threat of fever subsided, service further south resumed. By mid-November the bulletins announced that "Trains Nos. 1 and 4, which were annulled south of Birmingham, will be extended to Montgomery." The concern also threatened U.S. mail service that moved by rail. A London-based shipping paper reported that officials in New Orleans seriously considered "asking President McKinley to interfere for the purpose of maintaining mailing communication."[12]

The federal government and the American Public Health Association addressed the issue of the fever's dissemination via train while still allowing the railroad to function under trying circumstances. An examination of the guidelines established by the national authorities, however, underscored the difficulty of this assignment. For an inspection system to function, knowledgeable and preferably immune health inspectors required absolute authority and were posted inside and outside the trains. Travelers needed health certificates. Crew, passenger, and transfer lists were a must. The tramps drifting on freight cars required extra policing. The hoboes needed to be sequestered in observation camps, as opposed to being ejected with the "bum's rush" from a moving train.[13]

Cars with cane-backed seats were preferred over plush seats because fomites reportedly thrived in the upholstery. Sleeping cars were "more apt to get infected, as they are much harder to clean, contain infectious material, and moreover, being occupied at night on at least half the trains, they are very much apt to have cases of yellow fever develop in them." Hospital cars, isolation areas for rolling stock, physicians, and quarantine camps were also part of the arrangement.[14]

In the 1880s, Louisiana regained and strengthened its authority over the state quarantine stations. In 1886, the United States Supreme Court reversed the ruling of the Louisiana Supreme Court that
had prevented the state quarantine officials from collecting fees and policing trade in the case of *La. & Texas R.R. & S.S. Co. v. The Board of
Health of the State of Louisiana*. Holt, president of the Louisiana State
Board of Health from 1884 to 1888, promoted Louisiana as a world
leader in checking the importation of diseases with the "New System of
Maritime Sanitation" protection. Holt touted "The term MARITIME
SANITATION is of recent origin, and signifies the application of modern methods suggested by sanitary science and approved by experience in
the treatment of all carriers, persons, and things traversing the seas." Even
trade magazines such as *The Marine Journal* acknowledged Holt's expertise. When the doctor criticized the methods deployed battling yellow
fever in Jacksonville, Florida, the *Journal* noted "Dr. Holt's long experience and familiarity with the disease gives value to anything he may say
on this subject."[15]

In contrast, the century's last decade marked a reversal in the
gains made by the Louisiana Board of Health and the state's control of
hygiene responsibilities. Politicians, public health and business leaders,
and the general public that clamored for a consolidation of the quarantine authority advocated the continued decline in state authority. Despite
its flattering remarks concerning Holt, *The Marine Journal* called for "a
system of quarantine to be under the control of the [federal] Government through the marine hospital service." At the same time, native-born
Americans, who opposed the great influx of immigrants from Southern
and Eastern Europe, linked typhus and cholera to these new arrivals. The
nativists concluded that a permanent national quarantine policy might
stem the epidemical tide that struck cities in the northeastern United
States.[16]

In 1890, Congress granted to the Marine Hospital Service the
legal authority to establish an interstate federal quarantine system. Three
years later, Pres. Benjamin Harrison formalized this arrangement. The
federal government also sponsored yellow fever research. Continuing this
growing trend into the new century, in 1902, the Marine Hospital Service became the Public Health and Marine Hospital Service, and in 1912,

the organization simply became the Public Health Service. The actions instituted by Congress set the stage for the national authorities to play the major role in controlling the last yellow fever epidemic in Louisiana because the fever was recognized as a threat to the entire nation. Despite the recognized expertise in New Orleans, during the next epidemic, federal officials were well positioned to make the critical decisions.[17]

LOUISVILLE & NASHVILLE R. R. CO.

PASSENGER DEPARTMENT.

CIRCULAR No. 2133.
Supplement to No. 2132.

LOUISVILLE, KY., Nov 19, 1897.

YELLOW FEVER BULLETIN.

TO ALL CONCERNED:

Commencing this date, Trains Nos. 1 and 4, which were annulled south of Birmingham, will be extended to Montgomery, leaving Cincinnati 11:50 a. m., daily, and leaving Montgomery 9:40 p. m., daily.

On Monday, the 22d inst., through Sleeping-car line between Cincinnati and Jacksonville via Montgomery and the Plant System, on the trains referred to above, will be resumed.

General Passenger Agent.

Even relatively minor outbreaks of yellow fever could bring immediate and debilitating curtailments of commerce to and around New Orleans. In 1897, the Louisville and Nashville Railroad issued a string of yellow fever bulletins defining the restrictions and resumption of their limited services to the Deep South.

Throughout much of the 1880s and the early 1890s New Orleans enjoyed a respite from yellow jack. Despite the break, an 1893 city guide acknowledged that the city "is erroneously supposed to be the most unhealthy city in the United States." The guide also remarked "Yellow fever may now be considered stamped out, and will not appear again unless imported." Despite the guide's predictions, in 1897, the disease was imported, this time from Mississippi. Within the city, there were an estimated 2,000 cases that in resulted in 300 deaths. Surrounding communities isolated New Orleans with a ring of quarantines, and trade plummeted.[18]

According to Dr. Quitman Kohnke, New Orleans' health officer, the hint of an outbreak (that Kohnke was sure was not yellow fever) caused surrounding communities to quarantine against intercourse with New Orleans for ten days. From Kohnke's perspective, what others saw as a precaution was really an overreaction, and this response cost New Orleans "thousands and thousands of dollars on account of a false alarm." In that same time frame, Kohnke estimated the epidemic of 1897 cost the city about twenty million dollars.[19]

This epidemic proved that, although the number of outbreaks had declined, the city's association with the disease was as strong as ever, and competing trade centers were quick to exploit this morbid perception of New Orleans. The city fathers needed an anti-fever approach that eliminated the disease and undermined the quarantine tactics of nearby municipal and state governments. During the next and last epidemic to strike New Orleans, competing state governments turned to federal agencies to coordinate the campaign against the fever and do the bidding of their respective states.

Business leaders in New Orleans tried a number of approaches to return New Orleans to its antebellum status, while simultaneously reestablishing an effective and practical quarantine. Yellow jack, poor drainage, the lack of capital, and the destruction of the wharves by the caving riverbanks remained major stumbling blocks. To overcome these obstacles, the once-powerful New Orleans Chamber of Commerce united with the board of trade. Through unification, *The Marine News* hoped "that the new organization will enter upon a new and untiring effort to restore lost trade, open up and maintain new avenues of business, and succeed in placing New Orleans in the lines of other cities that have gotten the start of her growth and prosperity."[20]

In the latter half of the nineteenth century, there were general improvements in health care that benefited yellow fever victims. Physicians were less inclined to bleed patients or prescribe heroic doses of medications, especially mercury-based prescriptions. The nursing profession began to come into its own, and American medical schools elevated their curriculums and graduated more competent physicians. In addition, American physicians finally accepted that microorganisms were the cause of many diseases. On the downside, the number of spurious patent medicines available remained high. Fierce competition led to greater claims of various medicines' curative natures. The industry did not decline until after the passage of the Food and Drug Act of 1906 and rigorous prosecution of manufacturers for the false claims.

Despite the improvements in the field of medicine, so much of the city's fortune still appeared to be linked to the blessing of frost. An unidentified reporter for *The Marine Journal* discussing yellow fever drew upon his experience, and proclaimed a "black frost, [was] the only thing that could check" the fever. A black frost lacked the feathery, crystalline features of hoarfrost. Writing about the same time, Scotsman and Confederate veteran William Watson recalled differently that a "slight frost puts an end to the epidemic, but it also too often proves fatal to any one afflicted with it when the frost appears." So the aura of frost remained a visible omen.[21]

The century came to a close with the United States opening new markets through conquest. The Spanish-American War of 1898 afforded the victorious United States a unique opportunity to study yellow fever. Within a short span, yellow jack had killed far more American soldiers than had Spanish bullets. Following the conflict, the federal government sought to establish a global empire by assuming control of former Spanish colonies and building the Panama Canal. To accomplish this goal, a variety of exotic ailments needed to be overcome. Yellow fever was on the top of the list. Walter Reed headed an investigative team in Cuba later known as the Yellow Fever Commission. With encouragement from Dr. Carlos Juan Finlay of Cuba, and drawing upon breakthrough malaria research, the commission established that the *A. eygypti* was the sole vector. This supposition concerning the insect was dubbed the "mosquito theory."[22]

Yet, the military victory became a viral threat. The war heightened the fear that returning American troop ships would carry the fever from the West Indies to the United States. The year following the war, Dr. C.P. Wilkinson and his peers monitored fever epidemics in Vera Cruz, Mexico and Cuba while Wilkinson was stationed at Quarantine, Louisiana. He remarked to a South Carolina associate that while the current epidemic in Cuba had a high mortality rate, the reported figures were "compiled only from hospitals under special charge of Americans," and did not include records from private practice. Officials such as Wilkinson remained vigilant as yellow fever still had the power to create a national panic, strangle trade, and consume thousands of lives in a few short months. Wilkinson's vigilance was well justified. That same summer a soldier with yellow fever checked into the Southern Branch of the National Home for Disabled Volunteer Soldiers in Hampton, Virginia. The fever spread to forty-three inmates and claimed the lives of twelve. A hastily constructed self-imposed quarantine by the facility's officials kept the fever in check. Predictably, the surrounding communities established quarantines, and Baltimore blocked trade with all Virginia ports.[23]

Chapter Seven

THE MOSQUITO THEORY
AND THE EPIDEMIC OF 1905

Little Gold Locks has gone to bed,
Kisses are given and prayers are said,
Mamma says, as she turns out the light,
Mosquitoes wont bite my child to-night. *

In the fall of 1900, Walter Reed delivered the Yellow Fever Commission's preliminary findings to the American Public Health Association and published the results in *Philadelphia Medical Journal.* The following year in Havana, Reed also presented the commission's findings at the third Pan-American Medical Congress. After William C. Gorgas became convinced that Reed's conclusions were sound, Gorgas instituted a campaign to curtail yellow fever in Havana. He eliminated the water-retaining receptacles and other micro-environments that incubated mosquito larvae. His success in Cuba and later in Panama elevated himself and Reed to international heroes.[1]

Despite Gorgas's confirmation of the commission's findings, some Southerners did not accept Reed's conclusions. As a result, yellow fever still appeared occasionally in Southern ports. The Louisiana outbreak of 1905 was the last major occurrence in the United States. This reluctance of some officials and the general public is understandable given the endless number of false claims related to yellow fever that had preceded Reed's findings.[2]

As early as 1901, Dr. Quitman Kohnke, the chief New Orleans health officer, supported the mosquito theory. Furthermore, he organized an effort to blunt the insect's impact on the city. Kohnke designated an experimental zone to implement the measures needed to check mosquito reproduction. Teams fanned into the zone and informed the populace of the dangers of uncovered cisterns and freestanding water.

* Poem stanza from Clara Doty Bates, "The Cheated Mosquito," *St. Nicholas* 1 (September 1874): 640.

Despite Kohnke's hard work, the citizens did not embrace the spirit of the campaign. Without the backing of the masses, the municipal officials could not eliminate the multitude of containers that served as hatcheries for mosquito larva.[3]

The daunting undertaking of masking the estimated 75,000 cisterns faltered. Kohnke concluded, "Mosquitoes can be exterminated in a free country only by the co-operation, active or passive, of the people comprising the community; and to contribute this necessary acquiescence and assistance, they must first understand what is done, and why. If every man, woman, and child in this country understood the mosquito, legislative bodies would act in response to the general demand, and a concerted effort would soon accomplish with ease what, because of a lack of appreciation, promises to be a difficult and tedious task."[4]

South of New Orleans, the scenario in Cuba was favorable for such a labor-intensive public health undertaking. Reed and Gorgas worked in an environment tightly controlled by the federal government. In the United States, mandated plans did not meet with the same success because of a skeptical, diverse, and independent-thinking society. The converted medical professionals in New Orleans needed to convince the public of approximately 325,000 people that anti-mosquito controls merited their attention. Speculating that less than a quarter of this number had immunity to the fever, the public health leaders understood the ramifications of their life or death mission.[5]

One of the communities that contributed to the rich ethnic mix of New Orleans was the Italian immigrants. Ships from the Mediterranean Sea transported fruits, such as lemons, and seasonal male migrant workers to the state. The migrants harvested the sugar cane in the late fall. In New Orleans, the Italian community had been associated with the citrus fruit trade before the Civil War. Although many of the Sicilians departed the state after the cane harvest, others settled near the Old French Market area. At the beginning of the twentieth century, fruits from Central America and coffee from South America were critical trade commodities. New Orleans' access to the Midwest was an important feature of this enterprise. The Italians were closely linked to all of these commodities. Typically, the Italians owned groceries and small businesses, peddled produce, and labored as stevedores.[6]

Dr. C.B. White's report on carbolic acid sanitation in the 1870s gives insight into these immigrants' living conditions and how quickly the fever spread through a building. A thirty-room tenement of Chartres Street housed thirty families, totaling 183 people. Ninety-two residents were thought to be acclimated when forty-four residents contracted the fever. Of the forty-four, fourteen died, twenty-six recovered, and four were sent to the hospital; their fate is unknown.[7]

The Sicilians established close-knit communities thousands of miles from their homeland and practiced a code of silence. They considered the presence of municipal authority figures an intrusion. Catholicism, a part of Italian life, was already an integral part of the city, but there were nationalistic peculiarities involved in the same religion. Language differences between the white Southern Protestants and the Sicilians also created mutual distrust. Many native Southerners considered the Sicilians clannish and backward. The tension turned deadly when Italians thought to be part of organized crime were accused of killing a police official. Many defendants were exonerated only to be lynched. Betwixt this tense type of ethnic rift and urban violence, yellow fever surfaced.[8]

In May 1905, Italian stevedores probably contracted fever after unloading a shipment of bananas from Central America. Earlier that year, the disease was present in Belize and Panama. Although unfamiliar with yellow jack, all efforts to cure the disease were confined to the Italian community. As the virus spread, Sicilians fled the city and the state. Rumors of a "Roman fever" circulated. Living in dirty, crowded conditions, the Italians blamed the filthy gutters that city officials refused to clean despite numerous requests. The city still lacked a unified sanitation system and one estimate claimed the city had 13,688 blocks where water remained stagnant. Noteworthy among those that aided the Italians were the nuns associated with Mother Francesca Xavier Cabrini, the Missionary Sisters of the Sacred Heart. Mother Cabrini, who later became the first American saint, was not in the city at the time of the calamity. Archbishop Placide-Louis Chapelle, however, did return in late May from Havana to comfort his endangered flock. In the course of these duties, the archbishop contracted the fever and died in August.[9]

By mid-July, doctors saw suspicious cases, but city officials were not ready to announce the fever's presence until pathologists performed autopsies. In the meantime, word of the fever in New Orleans spread to Mississippi, where that state's secretary of the board of health asked Dr. Joseph H. White of the U.S. Public Health and Marine Hospital Service in Mobile to investigate the matter. White dispatched two experts to explore these allegations. An investigatory delegation from Alabama followed. After the examinations, on July 22, the city health officers announced that the deaths were caused by yellow fever, and three days later morbidity statistics revealed at least one hundred cases.[10]

On August 4, Louisiana Gov. Newton G. Blanchard telegraphed Pres. Theodore Roosevelt for assistance in curbing the fever. Roosevelt ordered the surgeon general to take action. Thus, White assumed overall control of the operations. White directed at least twenty-four public health officers and twenty-eight local civilian doctors. In executing their duties, some of the public health surgeons contracted the fever but they managed to subdue the fever.[11]

Screened Emergency Hospital Ambulance, New Orleans.

It was Kohnke's hope that this transfer of authority did not reflect the seriousness of the epidemic as much as it conveyed a good faith effort to instill confidence in communities outside of New Orleans. According to five-term Mayor Martin Behrman "our commercial rivals had in former years established quarantines on the slightest excuse [so] we stopped them by getting the federal government to take charge." The federal government required the state and city treasuries to subsidize the campaign against the fever. Once the national authorities moved to quell the epidemic the Louisiana politicians learned that they were not able to direct either the methods or extent of the federal involvement. Despite Behrman's wishful statement, state governments, such as Mississippi, established quarantines against Louisiana and also contacted the federal authorities to protect the citizens of their states.[12]

With the aid of Kohnke, White organized a massive campaign that educated the public, attacked the mosquito, eliminated breeding areas, fumigated and screened living quarters, and covered cisterns and privies. Kohnke allowed residents who could not screen their cisterns to temporarily deploy cheese cloth. Because oil on the surface of the water

Screening gang about to screen a room containing a yellow fever patient, New Orleans.

prevented the larvae from breathing on the surface, a teacup of insurance oil was added to the cisterns. Kohnke stressed "Yellow fever never was conveyed by filth, and never depended on dirt; it always depends on the conveyance of the germ by the particular mosquito." This was the message that he and his colleagues carried to the citizens.[13]

In the summer of 1905, with the fever in the city, Kohnke and White launched a beneficial educational program. Kohnke gave lantern slide lectures to local community groups. He also reached a national audience with his articles published in *Scientific American*. Religious, ethnic, and civic leaders took the word to their followers. Women's clubs organized their own house-to-house strategy to inform the populace. Dr. Felix Formento enlightened his fellow Italians in their native tongue. Political-style campaign buttons featured a mosquito in the center, surrounded by the words "My Cisterns are all right; How are Yours?" Kohnke tried to

Steam fumigating, New Orleans.

convince African Americans that it was also in their own best interests to participate in the drive, but black citizens were forced by whites to form their own ward-based organizations.[14]

The sick who had fled the French Market area were located, treated, and isolated behind netting and screens, so as not to come in contact with mosquitoes that might serve as new vectors of the disease. According to John Ellis, superintendent of Touro Infirmary, because of the net isolation method, he was able to inform his sister that "So far not a single case has developed in the hospital & not a day passes without our coming in direct contact & handling yellow fever cases. Isn't this a striking proof of the mosquito theory?"[15]

From the outset, Louisiana officials had been late communicating information about the possibility of a fever outbreak. In response, Gov. James K. Vardaman of Mississippi established a quarantine against New Orleans. Alabama, Texas, Georgia, southern Illinois, and other Louisiana municipalities followed the Magnolia State's lead. In 1884, the heads of the boards of health of gulf states and Tennessee had composed a written understanding concerning notification of actual or possible cas-

Fumigating gang at work, New Orleans.

es of epidemical diseases. The agreement also allowed for states to send representatives to explore the rumors of outbreaks "for the purpose of investigating and establishing the truth or falsity of such reports." When Louisiana was not forthcoming about the "suspicious" fever cases, the adjacent states were within their rights to send investigators and establish quarantines to protect their citizens.[16]

Not all outside localities, however, were pleased with the blockade. The resort towns of Pass Christian and Bay St. Louis in Mississippi

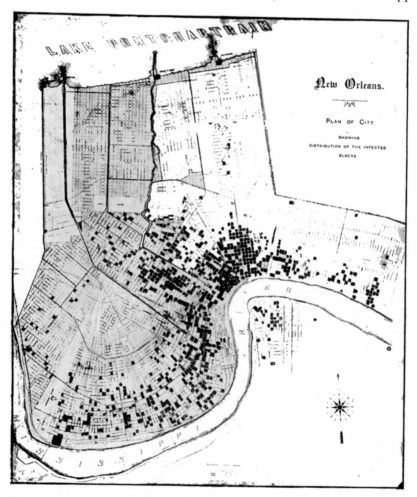

Mapping of the 1905 New Orleans yellow fever outbreak. Note the high concentration of cases in the Italian section of the lower French Quarter near the French Market.

relied heavily on vacationing citizens of New Orleans as part of their clientele. The town leaders of Pass Christian openly expressed their anti-quarantine views. They traveled to the state capitol in Jackson and lobbied to maintain contact with New Orleans even though they would be isolated from the rest of Mississippi.[17]

In contrast to Bay St. Louis, a few Louisiana communities reverted to the long-established shotgun quarantines. These vigilantes stopped outsiders from entering their respective town limits and prevented trains from stopping. Clinging to the belief that mail and packages spread yellow fever fomites, the town of Vinton disrupted mail service. To counter these disruptive and misplaced tactics, the federal government eliminated the post office in Vinton. Elsewhere in the state, travelers obtained certificates of health from local boards of health complete with physical descriptions of the traveler to facilitate non-infectious travel.[18]

Kohnke reacted strongly to the domestic quarantines against New Orleans and thought this was an overreaction to a problem well in hand. After the worst had passed, Kohnke noted how fear of yellow fever was unique among diseases. He concluded that "No one can imagine what panic is occasioned in the South whenever yellow fever occurs; typhoid can exist all over the country, and nobody seems to care very much about it, though it kills a great many people. Yellow fever cannot exist anywhere in the southern country without the whole world, apparently, knowing about it, and taking measures of precaution against it, out of all proportion to the seriousness of the disease and the danger of its conveyance."[19]

The reluctance of New Orleans' leaders to give timely and accurate information about the fever contributed to this reaction. Nonetheless, Kohnke's remarks are understandable when a few cases of fever were guaranteed to receive coverage in international commercial newspapers. For example, *Shipping Gazette & Lloyd's List Weekly Summary* in London reported early in 1905 that, "Eleven more deaths from yellow fever, including those reported for yesterday, and 32 fresh cases of disease, have been notified. The British ship *Bray Head* loaded at New Orleans and proceeded up the Mississippi [for] deck cargo of timber. Quarantine boats intervened and the *Bray Head* had to leave without the timber." It is interesting to note how this isolated occurrence related to yellow fever concerning an incoming bulk cargo vessel received attention in the European commercial press. Furthermore, it appears the crews of the quarantine boats acted correctly, but were still presented in a negative light.[20]

As mentioned, Louisiana was not the only state that turned to the federal government to protect its interests. In late July, Mississippi and Alabama supported the use of U.S. Revenue Cutter Service vessels and chartered launches to establish a yellow fever patrol. Moreover, the Louisiana governor accused the Mississippi militia and riverine patrols of being in cahoots with the Revenue Cutter Service by stopping domestic, fishing vessels within Louisiana waters, specifically Lake Borgne and the Rigolets Pass, and making inspections and towing the vessels to the Ship Island Quarantine Station. In a ranting telegraph to the secretary of the treasury, Gov. Newton C. Blanchard spouted that the Revenue Cutter Service had committed "an outrage on Louisiana" by coordinating with Mississippi patrol boats and escorting them to the quarantine station.[21]

Voicing the same frustrations as Louisiana's governor, the stockholders and the secretary of the Treasure Bay Oyster Company of New Orleans chided Lieut. S.P. Edmonds, the commanding officer of the *Winona*, for violating quarantine regulations. More importantly, the secretary claimed that while the Revenue Cutter Service was "safeguarding the public health, [the service still needed] to remove from commerce the shackles placed upon it by the fears born of ignorance, and to permit people of the state of Louisiana and the City of New Orleans to do all the business compatible with the safety of other communities."[22]

Lapel button used during the 1905 outbreak to promote the oiling and screening of cisterns.

The letter from the Treasure Bay Oyster Company to the Revenue Cutter Service graphically illustrates the tension between the local commercial interests and a federal agency involved with public safety. Unlike state organizations, however, the welfare of the Revenue

Cutter Service was not wed to the state. In addition, the federal government had sponsored the commission in Cuba that discovered the insect vector and benefited from the campaign that eliminated mosquito breeding environments in Havana. Armed with this knowledge during the last epidemic, the federal government finally assumed the authority and responsibility to impose its will on New Orleans and place the well being of the nation before the interests of Louisiana.

Poster issued at New Orleans during the 1905 yellow fever outbreak, the last significant appearance of the disease in the United States.

Despite this perceived infringement on Louisiana's sovereignty by a federal agency normally focused on international trade, the inspections continued even without the support of the U.S. Public Health and Marine Hospital Service in New Orleans. The Revenue Cutter Service did receive the cooperation of federal public health officials on Ship Island. Those revenue steamers and schooners involved in the patrol made daily written reports to the U.S. secretary of the treasury, Leslie M. Shaw. Ad-

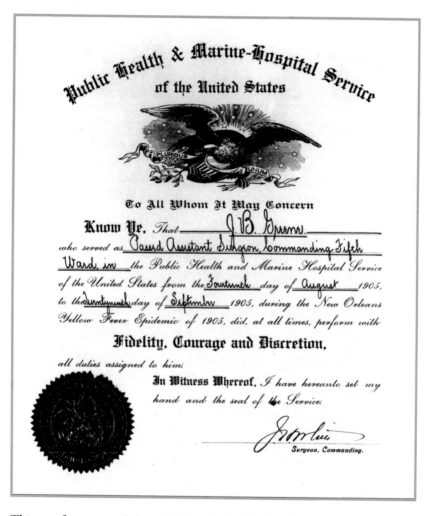

This certificate, awarded in 1905 by the Public Health and Marine Hospital Service, was part of the federal government's increased role in protecting the public's health on an international scale. Image courtesy of the Mariners' Museum Library and Archives, Newport News, VA.

ditionally, Shaw assumed that the federal quarantine law of 1893 gave the Revenue Cutter Service the authority to support state quarantines. The secretary of treasury's reaction to this "misunderstanding of the source of authority directing the actions of these patrol boats in Louisiana waters, and the menace to commerce of the existing rules" was to send Capt. Worth G. Ross to take command of the patrol fleet. Clearly, once the federal authorities mobilized to check the fever, the state of Louisiana surrendered control of the situation.[23]

In early September 1905, Ross reported that over an eight-day span thirty-seven vessels had been disinfected at Ship Island. This group included six schooners and a motorboat from New Orleans. The dispatches to Shaw reported violations and the appearance of yellow fever in Gulfport, Mississippi, causing Ross to suspend liberty for the patrol boats' crews.[24]

Looking beyond their differences with Mississippi, New Orleans officials knew that the American public would base the severity of the fever on the reaction of the city's citizens. Therefore, the local Elks Club proceeded with a Diamond Parade. The festivities were a fundraiser for yellow fever relief but also projected an upbeat image while combating

OFFICE OF BOARD OF HEALTH

CERTIFICATE OF HEALTH.

Wisner ...... La., *Aug. 13*, 1905

To Whom It May Concern:

This is to Certify, That the bearer *Mrs. Allen Phillips* of *Manfield* ...is in good health and has given satisfactory evidence that *she* has not been in contact with *yellow fever* ...or any contagious disease.

Description: Race *white* age *43* height *5. 6* weight *134*

color of hair .... color of eyes *gray*

.... M. D.
Health Officer.

This descriptive certificate of health, issued on August 13, 1905, at Wisner in northwestern Louisiana, allowed the assignee to move within the state at a time when certain travel was restricted and the fear of spreading yellow fever outside New Orleans was at its highest.

the fever. The celebration included contests, baseball games, and a grand march. In the procession, one of the Elks carried a banner that proclaimed "AND IT HAD TO BE A FEMALE!" in reference to the female mosquito spreading yellow fever. Other club members sported costumes of "cheese cloth and [wore] hats [that were] good imitations of screened cisterns."[25]

The success of White and the Public Health and Marine Hospital Service secured the future of the agency and justified federal control of the quarantine stations. On the local level, Mayor Behrman recalled, "I think we were slow in adopting the screening and oiling. It should have been done before, But we made up for lost time as best we could and when netting gave out we used cheese clothe [*sic*] for screens."[26] The former mayor made no mention about the delay in reporting suspicious fever cases to neighboring states.

Scientific American echoed Behrman's sentiments in a piece published while the efforts to control the threat were ongoing. The article also spoke of the conversion of the governors of Mississippi and Louisiana to the mosquito theory and delivered a backhanded compliment to the Italians:

TOURO INFIRMARY

In 1882 the second Touro Infirmary building was dedicated. The structure was slated for demolition in June 1905, but New Orleans' last significant outbreak of yellow fever delayed demolition until the fall of that year. Because of the main building's inaccessibility, staff treated patients in the administrative building during the epidemic. Image courtesy of the Touro Infirmary Archives, New Orleans, LA.

Perhaps no better instance of the good work accomplished in a sanitary and educational way could be shown than in the case of the Italians. These people, among whom the fever started, and whom have been its worst victims, were the bane of the local health officials at the beginning of the epidemic; so much so that the towns prohibited the incoming of any Italians and some even ejected them. Yet the Italians, who constituted nine-tenths of the cases and deaths at the beginning of the epidemic, constitute only a fraction to-day; the Italian quarter is nearly free from fever and is cleaner than it has ever been or believed it could be. Those who thought it impossible to teach the lower class of Sicilians the value of cleanness find themselves mistaken.

These condescending remarks were typical for the times and explain how the schism between the rising immigrant population and

This interior view of the charity ward of Touro Infirmary reveals tubing above the beds that could have served as framework for mosquito bars. Image courtesy of the Touro Infirmary Archives, New Orleans, LA.

established American communities flourished and allowed the epidemic to gain a foothold. In that same vein, Italians had been singled out by the Baton Rouge quarantine and prevented from seeking refuge in the state capital during the epidemic.[27]

The citywide battle against the mosquito during the epidemic of 1905 did not convince all medical professionals and the general public that the campaign against the *A. aegypti* had terminated the yellow fever threat. For instance, while he did not refute that mosquitoes carried the virus, Dr. Reginald Leech was convinced that the monumental task of screening the cisterns was not the cause of the abatement of the fever. Leech claimed the fever still raged after the covering and draining efforts started and the task of effectively reducing the number of mosquitoes was too great an undertaking.

Instead, Leech advocated that the wholesale consumption of 100,000 lots of arsenious-acid tablets in twenty-three days was the true reason for the termination of the epidemic. Leech claimed that only five of the 165,000 "arsenicized persons" contracted yellow jack. Although arsenic was recognized as a poison, it also had long been prescribed for intermittent fevers. The popularity of the pills indicated the resilient popularity of patent medicines with people hedging their bets by screening their cisterns and ingesting the tablets.[28]

On the heels of the Public Health Service and the Revenue Cutter Service, in late October, Theodore Roosevelt answered the call to visit New Orleans and arrived in grand style on the *U.S.S. West Virginia*. Earlier in his exciting career, he had flirted with yellow fever as a leader of the Rough Riders in the Spanish-American War. Against the reservations of his advisors, he again tempted death when he toured the Crescent City as part of a regional jaunt. Roosevelt had alienated white Southerners by his progressive stand on race issues, but he used the tour as an opportunity to mend fences in Dixie.

The citizens of New Orleans applauded the popular president at every function. The only time the president appeared in danger occurred when the lighthouse tender that ferried him to his flagship collided with a fruit steamer. The president and his entourage were unharmed. Roosevelt took advantage of the opportunity the epidemic offered to demonstrate both his courage and compassion.[29]

Roosevelt and New Orleans mutually benefited from the visit. Mayor Behrman understood the public relations value of the trip when the mayor concluded "it would have taken years of 'press agent' work to get the results we got through Roosevelt's visit." As for Roosevelt, he was able to demonstrate the type of fearless character in the face of the fever that had made the careers of Southern politicians. Unrecognized by the mayor, Roosevelt's presence also symbolized the rise of the federal government in public health and quarantine matters and the decline of intrastate squabbling.[30]

The lessons learned in the last yellow fever epidemic came at a considerable loss of life. There were approximately 3,400 cases of yellow fever, 452 of which proved fatal. Across Louisiana more than 9,300 people contracted the disease. Finally though, the public became convinced that one of the critical mysteries involving the fever had been identified and understood their role in curbing the scourge. John Ellis touted "'Yellow Jack' is not what it used to be and [it will] be the last epidemic in America. There may be a few imported cases but it will never gain a foot hold [*sic*] . . . New Orleans will be practically rebuilt—in fact the process is well under way. . . . It's a wonder the whole city has not died out before."[31]

Ellis's predictions came true. New Orleans is one of the busiest ports in the United States and one the great tourist destinations of the world. Today, tourists, revelers, and conventioneers arrive all year round without fear of the fever. As for the frost, on October 13, 1905, the *Daily Picayune* ran a cartoon that depicted the North Wind sending a mosquito packing with the chilly wind generated from hand bellows. The caption read "FAREWELL FOREVER!" Now, however, convinced that the mosquito was the pathogen's vector, the residents of New Orleans did not have to flee or await the blessing of frost to combat the plight of yellow fever.[32]

FAREWELL FOREVER!

Note the bag carried by the female mosquito labeled "Mme. Stegomyia." At the time of this last outbreak, the yellow fever mosquito's scientific name was *Stegomyia fasciata*.

EPILOGUE AND A PERSONAL NOTE

The study of humankind's desire to conquer yellow fever is fascinating. The story has all the twists of a good mystery novel. Plot lines show how diligent scientists identified the true vectors of yellow fever, only to be ignored by colleagues. Conversely, well-founded hypotheses were not rigorously tested and therefore went unproven for decades. The number of false claims concerning yellow fever's causes and cures were so numerous that, when the right answers unfolded, it took years to convince the populace that a critical piece of the puzzle truly had been located.

At the same time, ancient assumptions widely accepted by the medical profession proved costly in lives and trade. The belief in nebulous fomites and the practice of bleeding come to mind. Equally intriguing were the rational decisions made on the false assumption that the fever was linked to poor sanitation. General Butler's drive to clean Southern cities stands as the best example of this misplaced effort. Just as intriguing is the development of meteorological monitoring with the expectation that associated disease patterns would emerge. The arguments revolving around yellow fever give insight into the belief systems of nineteenth-century American medical science and the reluctance of the skeptical public to totally embrace their opinions and theories.

Yellow fever epidemics exposed the gamut of human nature. Thieves preyed on the sick. Parents abandoned sick children to save themselves and their surviving offspring. African Americans held the community together while at the same time slaves fled to freedom. Clergy members, doctors, and municipal officials built their reputations on their willingness to face the scourge. When the fever passed, kind volunteers gathered the orphans to find them new homes. And even in the tense years before and after the Civil War, Northern citizens gave hundreds of thousands of dollars and an endless stream of supplies to their fever-racked brethren in the South.

Throughout the century, yellow jack's aura contributed to the unsavory reputation of Southern ports with New Orleans at center stage of this horrific drama. The municipality was hailed as the Queen City of the South, and, at the same time, called the Calcutta of America. The impact of the virus also spread across the region. As a result, historian David K. Patterson has concluded yellow fever "was one of the diseases which not only helped to shape the image of the South as the poor, backward part of the nation, but also helped to create that reality."[1]

In reference to yellow fever, New Orleans has a number of unwanted distinctions. In 1853, more people died in the prevailing epidemic than in any single outbreak. In 1878, the nation's worst epidemic originated in the Crescent City. The citizens endured the highest number of serious outbreaks, and, in 1905, the last epidemic in the United States. Ten years after the last outbreak, Louisiana author Grace King described the gruesome pallor generated by yellow fever as "Death, as palpable, visible, as a stolid official executioner; and not as a fleeting presence but functioning steadily, regularly for days, weeks, months, year after year."[2]

Although not an imminent threat to the United States, yellow fever still has the ability to worry public health authorities. One of the mysteries involving yellow fever concerns a potential for an outbreak in the world's most populated countries. Why the fever does not appear in Asia and the Pacific Rim is not clear. In the early 1900s, there was legitimate concern that the opening of the Panama Canal would transport wave after wave of the dreaded pestilence to China, India, and Japan.[3]

Likewise, beginning in the 1980s, events caused world health officials to give yellow fever a wary second look. Insecticide-resistant mosquitoes, the transferring of invasive species of mosquitoes to new environments, the ban on the insecticide DDT, global warming, human encroachment upon rain forests, and a steady stream of international flights may have all contributed to the reemergence of mosquito-borne diseases. Specifically, Dr. Susan E. Robertson and her colleagues of the World Health Organization observed "*Aedes aegypti* mosquitoes are now present in urban areas in the Americas (including southern parts of the United States), and there is concern that yellow fever could erupt in explosive outbreaks."[4]

The public concern about mosquitoes and related pathogens is reflected in the contents of the *National Geographic* and *Discover* magazines. Recent articles in these magazines emphasize the rise of mosquito-borne diseases and the innovative means of controlling the pathogen.

For instance, Alexander Raikhel and Vladimir Kokoza of Michigan State University hope to develop a strain of mosquitoes that will digest the life-threatening viruses once the viruses are ingested. Currently, the pathogens are able to survive within the mosquitoes. If, however, the mosquitoes digest the harmful virus, the pathogen will not be passed to humans when the mosquitoes seek their next blood meals.[5]

In the 1990s, two men unknowingly brought yellow fever into the United States. In 1996, a man in Tennessee died of yellow fever. This occurrence was chilling to students of history who recalled that, in the 1870s, the fever repeatedly decimated the citizens of Memphis. The victim had taken a brief trip to the rain forests of Brazil but failed to get the recommended immunization. He was ill upon his return and expired "days after hospital admission and [ten] days after the onset of symptoms." Three years later, a man returning from Venezuela to California died of yellow fever under circumstances similar to the Tennessee victim. As the use of air travel continues to grow, this type of isolated occurrence may develop into a pattern.[6]

Reminiscent of yellow jack was the appearance of West Nile fever. In 1999, the virus appeared in New York. In a few years, the mosquito-borne virus spread across most of the nation. The virus has been found in ten species of mammals and at least one hundred bird species, and this number is rising. Some of the birds migrate; others are permanent residents. In addition, there are at least eleven species of mosquito that can carry the virus. It should be noted that many of the humans who contract the disease exhibit flu-like or no symptoms of the illness (defined as West Nile fever or WNF). Among a few individuals, however, the West Nile virus (WNV) can cause encephalitis, meningitis, paralysis, and even death.

In response to the fever's presence in 2002, the Louisiana Office of Public Health launched the "Fight The Bite" campaign. Authorities advised citizens to get rid of old tires and water-holding containers, fill small puddles and hollow stumps, change the water in bird baths, wear light clothing and long sleeves, and repair door and window screens. The list of directives echoed early twentieth-century efforts to cover cisterns and eliminate freestanding water. Fueling the public consternation were stories in national dailies such as *USA Today* proclaiming "La. Feverish with West Nile worry: 5 deaths linked to virus carried by mosquitoes; residents living in the state of emergency." By the end of the year, the Centers for Disease Control reported more than 300 WNV cases, and nineteen deaths in the state. Fatefully, Louisiana was among the states with both high morbidity and mortality rates. More than any other pathogen, WNV has reminded the American populace of the potentially deadly combination of mosquitoes and viruses.[7]

Similarly, in the spring of 2003, the Severe Acute Respiratory Syndrome (SARS) first surfaced in Hong Kong and other parts of China. Soon, isolated cases quickly appeared around the globe. National medical agencies accused Chinese authorities of not correctly reporting the scope of the ailment. As a result, the Chinese once again projected the old image of a secretive, sequestered nation, and not the persona of a burgeoning global player Beijing now fosters. To counter the criticism, the Communist Party removed two major officials, the mayor of Beijing and minister of health from office. *Washington Post* called the dramatic move "the most significant political shake-up in more than a decade." The concern continued into the fall, as officials moved the women's World Cup soccer tournament from China to the United States.[8]

The SARS scare prompted tourists and business associates to cancel flights to Asia. This reaction hurt not only Asian manufacturers but also the struggling airlines. In the West, businesses in the numerous Chinatowns felt the loss of retail trade even though no early cases of SARS had been reported in these communities. Alert authorities in California isolated aircraft with passengers from Asia who claimed to be feeling ill in an attempt to keep the virus in check. With Asia being the dynamo that produces a variety of manufactured goods for the world economy, every nation felt the pinch.

Decades before the appearance of SARS and WNF in North America, I had my first brush with yellow fever. My father was a naval officer, and he had received orders for a duty station on the island of Trinidad in the West Indies. Before making the transfer, my family traveled weekly to the dispensary at the Yorktown Naval Weapons Station for about two months to endure the gauntlet of necessary inoculations. One of those shots was for yellow fever.

Once on the island, I was fascinated with the wildlife. From my youthful point of view, the frogs were the size of rats and the rats the size of cats. Beautiful butterflies, bats, huge ant colonies, tarantulas, scorpions, boas, iguanas, and stories of the menacing barracudas added to the wonderful menagerie. In considering the animals, I was told that some of the "monkeys" had been killed because they spread diseases. Naturally, I was distressed at this pronouncement. Nevertheless, I could hear howler monkeys in the bamboo forests, and I was thrilled early one evening when a Marine officer showed me a mother howler and her young offspring moving high among the bamboo.

It was not until thirty-five years later that I learned about a yellow fever outbreak on Trinidad in 1954. Attempts to control the primate population would have been part of a plan to eliminate the reservoir of the virus found in the primates in the sylvan environment. Having written this book, I now understand the need to make those weekly trips to get all those painful shots and the efforts to control the primate population. Still, I was also happy to get glimpse at those howlers that vocalized their presence at night in the mysterious "jungle" of my backyard.

In the final month of preparing this manuscript for printing, Hurricane Katrina ravaged the Gulf Coast. The parallels of the storm and the yellow fever epidemics of the region are extremely disturbing. The unattended dead seen on television are stark reminders of what happens when the sinews of order snap. Just as remarkable, Americans have donated hundreds of millions of dollars and the figure is still rising. As with other disasters, the issues of class, race, regionalism, and ethnicity are critical to understanding the situation and continue to cloud discussions of relief, response, and the responsibility for individuals and governments. Ten of thousands citizens fled from Katrina and yellow jack. In both of these instances, the poor and the sick had limited options and resources.

In the summer of 1905, the leadership of Louisiana asked for the federal government's assistance in fighting the country's last fever epidemic. The national government did respond but not always to the liking of Louisianans. Still, Pres. Theodore Roosevelt scored points with his visit to New Orleans in the last days of the epidemic and was lionized by the Crescent City public. A century later the city again turned to the federal government for help. In contrast to Roosevelt's visit, Pres. George W. Bush's speech from New Orleans received mixed reviews and he has been sharply criticized for the federal government's response. With no general public in the city to respond to Bush's remarks and promises, the president aimed his words at an international audience. Despite his acknowledgment of the federal government's inadequate response to this disaster, critics have not stopped blaming the federal government, state and local bureaucrats, and law enforcement officers for their late and often ineffective response.

As I write, the story of Katrina unfolds by the minute and invites comparisons to the past. A few moments ago, the head of Charity Hospital stated that the facility is inhabitable and must be rebuilt. With that remark, I think of the first time the hospital was rebuilt after a hurricane. That effort took time, but Charity was reborn. In lean and fat times, this institution has been the last beacon of hope to the city's poor and is a critical part of the underpinning of the state for many of its citizens.

In dark times pensive historians are extremely reluctant to make predictions, but certainly the debate of disaster relief will become a political football. As during yellow fever epidemics, elected officials will have to answer for their decisions before the hurricane and lay bare their actions in Katrina's aftermath. Finger-pointing, so much a part of the landscape in all disasters, will continue for decades. On a higher note, I am confident that heroes not yet recognized will emerge as part of the lore of the region and nation. The spirit of the Howard Association has well been represented by anonymous medical personnel, law enforcement officers, firefighters, humanitarians, and members of the armed forces.

Beyond Katrina, it appears that the steady surge in hurricane activity in the early twenty-first century has replaced yellow fever as the scourge of the southeastern coast of the United States. Northeast of the Gulf of Mexico, (as I am reshaping these closing paragraphs, the residents along North Carolina's Outer Banks begin to repair the serious damage left by a slow-moving, category one hurricane named Ophelia). A few days later, Louisianians, Texans, and tourists of the Florida Keys were required to evacuate because the awesome power of Hurricane Rita. Having long shook the pall of yellow fever, Gulf Coast Orleans has grown to depend on the tourist and convention-goers for its economic survival, yet travelers such as these may find other destinations that offer a greater comfort level.

In conclusion, I wonder not so much when, but just how the Big Easy will return, and what has already been lost forever. This exotic city has drawn me for more than twenty years as a conventioneer, sports fan, history student, and reveler. The continuation of my relationship, as well as countless others, may affect the future of the city. Both the gulf residents and the nation's citizens want to rebuild New Orleans. The rebuilders may be new arrivals but the city will rebound. And in this Janus-faced prediction is an echo of remarks of Mississippi River man Cap. Samuel Cumings observing with wonder the eclectic masses that found their way to New Orleans to make their fortune.

Benjamin H. Trask
York County, Virginia
September 2005

NOTES
TO CHAPTER ONE

[1] Samuel Cumings, *The Western Pilot; Containing Charts of the Ohio River and of the Mississippi* (Cincinnati, 1834), 119.

[2] Khaled J. Bloom, *The Mississippi Valley's Great Yellow Fever Epidemic of 1878* (Baton Rouge, 1993), 2; Ralph Chester Williams, *The United States Public Health Service, 1798-1950* (Washington, D.C., 1951), 115; Jo Ann Carrigan, "Yellow Fever Scourge of the South" in Todd L. Savitt and James Harvey Young, eds., *Disease and Distinctiveness in the American South* (Knoxville, TN, 1988), 66; Quitman Kohnke, "The Mosquito Question," *Scientific American Supplement* 59 (1905): 243-46.

[3] Rudolph Matas, "A Yellow Fever Retrospect and Prospect," *Louisiana Historical Quarterly* 8 (July 1925): 458; L. H. Collier and Moray C. Timbury, eds., *Topley & Wilson's Principles of Bacteriology, Virology and Immunity*, 5 vols. (Philadelphia, 1990), 4:582-83; Deanne Nuwer, "The 1878 Yellow Fever Epidemic of Mississippi" (Ph.D. dissertation, University of Southern Mississippi, 1996), 7-13.

[4] Gordon McPherson, ed., *Black's Medical Dictionary* (Lanham, MD, 1999), 594-95; Kenneth F. Kiple, ed., *The Cambridge World History of Human Disease* (Cambridge, England, 1993), 592-93, 1102.

[5] Mark Twain, "The Metropolis of the South," in Etolia S. Basso, ed., *The World From Jackson Square: A New Orleans Reader* (New York, 1948), 266-67.

[6] James D. Goodyear, "The Sugar Connection: A New Perspective on the History of Yellow Fever," *Bulletin of the History of Medicine* 52 (Spring 1978): 11-13; John A. Heitmann, *The Modernization of the Sugar Industry, 1830-1910* (Baton Rouge, 1987), 13-14; David K. Patterson, "Yellow Fever Epidemics and Mortality in the United States, 1693-1905," *Social Science & Medicine* 34 (April 1992): 855-60.

[7] Erasmus Darwin Fenner, *History of the Epidemic Yellow Fever at New Orleans, Louisiana in 1853* (New York, 1854), 49-53; Wilbur G. Downs, "History of Epidemiological Aspects of Yellow Fever," *Yale Journal of Biology and Medicine* 55 (1982): 179.

[8] Dale A. Somers, ed., "New Orleans At War: A Merchant's View," *Louisiana History* 14 (1973): 55 (quotation, p. 56); Patterson, "Yellow Fever Epidemics," 855-60 (quotation, p. 860).

[9] Jo Ann Carrigan, *The Saffron Scourge: A History of Yellow Fever in Louisiana, 1796-1905* (Lafayette, LA, 1994), 17-19, 22-28.

[10] Jack D.L. Holmes, "The New Orleans Yellow Fever Epidemic of 1796 As Seen By the Baron de Pontalba," *Alabama Journal of Medical Sciences* 2 (1965): 205-14 (quotation, p. 209).

131

[11] Laura L. Porteous, trans., "Sanitary Conditions in New Orleans Under the Spanish Regime, 1799-1800," *Louisiana Historical Quarterly* 15 (1932): 612-15; James Pitot, *Observations on the Colony of Louisiana from 1796 to 1802* (Baton Rouge, 1979), 111.

[12] Harold D. Langley, *A History of Medicine in the Early U.S. Navy* (Baltimore, 1995), 108-11; Jon Kukla, *A Wilderness So Immense: The Louisiana Purchase and the Destiny of America* (New York, 2003), 222-24.

[13] Dunbar Rowland, ed., *Official Letter Books of W.C.C. Claiborne, 1801-1816*, 6 vols. (Jackson, MS, 1917), 2:307, 314, 337 (first quotation, p. 306; second quotation, p. 328; third quotation, p. 352); John A. Garraty and Mark C. Carnes, eds., *American National Biography*, 24 vols. (New York, 1999) 4:895-96; Langley, *Medicine in the Early U.S. Navy*, 108-11; Robert Florence, *New Orleans Cemeteries: Life in the Cities of the Dead* (New Orleans, 1997), 56.

[14] Pitot, *Colony of Louisiana*, xx-xxi, 110-12 (quotation, p. 105).

[15] Walter Prichard, ed., "Three Letters of Richard Claiborne to William Miller, 1816-1818," *Louisiana Historical Quarterly* 24 (1941): 739; "Yellow Fever in New Orleans and Mortality of New York," *Illustrated London News* 23 (September 10, 1853): 263; Earl F. Niehaus, "The New Irish, 1830-1862," in Carl A. Brasseaux, ed., *A Refuge For All Ages: Immigration in Louisiana History*, vol. 10, *Louisiana Purchase Bicentennial Series in Louisiana History* (Lafayette, LA, 1996), 378.

[16] Edward C. Carter, II, et al., eds., T*he Journals of Benjamin Henry Latrobe 1799-1820: From Philadelphia to New Orleans*, 3 vols. (Baltimore and New Haven, 1980), 3:311; John C. Van Horne, ed., *The Correspondence and Miscellaneous Papers of Benjamin Henry Latrobe*, 3 vols. (Baltimore and New Haven, 1988), 3:1036; *The State of the Union: Being a Complete Documentary History of the Public Affairs of the United States Foreign and Domestic, for the Year 1854* (Washington, D.C., 1855), 168.

[17] David T. Gleeson, *The Irish in the South, 1815-1877* (Chapel Hill, N.C., 2001), 45-6.

[18] Langley, *Medicine in the Early U.S. Navy*, 118-20.

[19] Ibid., 122-23; *American National Biography*, 4:896; Rowland, *W.C.C. Claiborne* vol. 2: 369 (all quotations, p. 363).

[20] Thomas Ashe, *Travels in America, Performed in 1806*, 3 vols. (London, 1808), 3:255-56 (quotation from p. 242).

[21] *The American Almanac and Repository of Useful Knowledge for the Year 1831* (Boston, 1830), 241.

[22] Langley, *Medicine in the Early U.S. Navy*, 16-17; Robert Straus, *Medical Care For Seamen: The Origin of the Public Medical Service in the United States* (New Haven, CT, 1950), 1-15.

[23] Langley, *Medicine in the Early U.S. Navy*, 109-11; Straus, *Medical Care For Seamen*, 36-37.

[24] "The New Orleans Charity Hospital," *Harper's Weekly* 3 (September 3, 1859): 569-70; John Salvaggio, *New Orleans' Charity Hospital: A Story of Physicians, Politics, and Poverty* (Baton Rouge, 1992), 9, 22-25, 39-40, 47-49.

[25] Maunsel White, "The Olden Time in New-Orleans and Yellow Fever," *De Bow's Commercial Review of the South and West* 6 (August 1846): 136-38.

[26] Carter, *Journals of Benjamin H. Latrobe*, 3:314-15.

[27] Cumings, *Western Pilot*, 119; Rowland, *W.C.C. Claiborne*, 2:352.

[28] Prichard, "Three Letters of Richard Claiborne," 739.

[29] Thomas E. Redard, "The Port of New Orleans: An Economic History, 1821-1850," 2 vols. (Ph.D. dissertation, Louisiana State University, 1985), 1:34; David R. Goldfield, "The Business of Health Planning: Disease Prevention in the Old South," *Journal of Southern History* 42 (1976): 560.

[30] Carter, *Journals of Benjamin H. Latrobe*, 3:312; John Duffy, *Sword of Pestilence: The New Orleans Yellow Fever Epidemic of 1853* (Baton Rouge, 1966), 3-12, 16-17; Margaret Humphreys, *Yellow Fever and the South* (New Brunswick, N.J., 1992), 60; John H. Ellis, *Yellow Fever & Public Health in the New South* (Lexington, KY, 1992), 33.

[31] Savoie Lottinville, ed., *Paul Wilhelm, Duke of Württemberg: Travels in North America, 1822-1824* (Norman, OK, 1973), 34.

[32] James H. Dormon, Jr., *Theater in the Ante Bellum South, 1815-1861* (Chapel Hill, 1967), 65, 78; P.T. Barnum, *Struggles and Triumphs; on Forty Years' Recollections of P.T. Barnum* (Buffalo, 1873), 103, 329, 353-54; Flora Bassett Hildreth, "The Howard Association of New Orleans, 1837-1878" (Ph.D. dissertation, University of California-Los Angeles, 1978), 94; "Miss Jenny Lind," *Sailor's Magazine and Naval Journal* 23 (1851): quotation, p. 348.

[33] Carter, *Journals of Benjamin H. Latrobe*, 3:305-14 (first quotation, p. 306; second quotation, p. 307).

[34] Samuel Wilson, Jr., ed., *Southern Travels: Journal of John H.B. Latrobe* (New Orleans, 1986), 1; Horne, *Correspondence of Benjamin H. Latrobe*, 3:945.

[1] George Wilson Pierson, *Tocqueville in America* (Baltimore and London, 1996), 625 and 627; Henry Tudor, *Narrative of a Tour in North America*, 3 vols. (London, 1834), 2:64.

[2] Theodore Clapp, *Autobiographical Sketches and Recollections during a Thirty-Five Years' Residence in New Orleans* (Boston, 1857), 189.

[3] Ibid., 85; Mary E. Stovall, "'To Be, To Do, and To Suffer': Responses to Death in the Nineteenth-Century Central South," *Journal of Mississippi History* 52 (1990): 97

[4] A. Oakey Hall, *The Manhattaner in New Orleans: or Phases of "Crescent City" Life*, ed. Henry A. Kmen (Baton Rouge, 1976), xiii-xxvi.

[5] Ibid., 69.

[6] Wilson, *Journal of John H.B. Latrobe*, 1 (quotations pp. 86-87); *Dictionary of American Biography* (New York, 1933), 9:20-8.

[7] James Stuart, *Three Years in North America*, 3 vols. (Edinburg, 1833), 1:229, 230.

[8] Burton Randall to My Brother, November 4, 1833, Randall Family Papers, Special Collections, Small Library, University of Virginia.

[9] Hildreth, "The Howard Association," 59, 74-5; Robert Baird, *Impressions and Experiences of the West Indies and North America in 1849* (Philadelphia, 1850), 192; Carrigan, *Saffron Scourge*, 55.

[10] Langley, *Medicine in the Early U.S. Navy*, 108-11; "Report on the Subject of Marine Hospitals," *Report of the Secretary of the Treasury*, 31st Congress, 2d Session, Ex. Doc. No. 14 [Senate], January 20, 1851; Straus, *Medical Care For Seamen*, 52-54.

[11] James R. Fleming, *Meteorology in America, 1800-1870* (Baltimore, 1990), xvii, 61-62, 68-73.

[12] Florence, *New Orleans Cemeteries*, 24-29, 53.

[13] William L. Robinson, *The Diary of a Samaritan* (New York, 1860), 18, 72.

[14] Hildreth, "Howard Association," 1, 226; Charles Gardner, comp., *Gardner & Wharton's New Orleans Directory, for the Year 1858* (New Orleans, 1857), 390.

[15] Jonathan B. Pritchett and İnsan Tunali, "'Strangers' Disease': Determinants of Yellow Fever Mortality during the New Orleans Epidemic of 1853," *Explo-*

rations in Economic History 32 (1995): 522, 526-27; Donald E. Everett, "The New Orleans Yellow Fever Epidemic of 1853," *Louisiana Historical Quarterly* 33 (1950): 393.

[16] Salvaggio, *Charity Hospital*, 74; Fenner, *Yellow Fever at New Orleans, 1853*, 57; Everett, "Yellow Fever Epidemic of 1853," 385.

[17] Salvaggio, *Charity Hospital*, 31; Kay K. Moss, *Southern Folk Medicine, 1750-1820* (Columbia, S.C., 1999), 30, 219-20; Egbert Guernsey, *Homoepathic* [sic] *Domestic Practice: Containing also Chapters On Physiology, Hygiene, Anatomy, and An Abridged Materia Medica* (New York, 1860), quotation, p. 25.

[18] Carrigan, *Saffron Scourge*, 248, 269-70; Karl T. Weber, "Let's clear the air of that nocturnal miasma. Cigar anyone?" *Cardiovascular Research* 37 (1998): 7.

[19] J. Worth Estes, *Dictionary of Protopharmacology: Therapeutic Practices, 1700-1850* (Canton, MA, 1990), 34; Judith Lee Hollock, "'Lethal and Debilitating': The Southern Disease Environment as a Factor In Confederate Defeat," *Journal of Confederate History* 7 (1991): 61.

[20] Estes, *Dictionary of Protopharmacology*, 47-49, 106; Moss, *Southern Folk Medicine*, 190, 194.

[21] Moss, *Southern Folk Medicine*, 30, 219-20; Liliane Crété, *Daily Life in Louisiana, 1815-1830* (Baton Rouge, 1978), 195.

[22] R. Eglesfeld Griffith, *A Universal Formulary: Containing the Methods of Preparing and Administering Officinal and Other Medicines* (Philadelphia, 1850), 476-78; Moss, *Southern Folk Medicine*, 20, 30-34.

[23] Danforth P. Wight, *Seaman's Guide, Containing the Symptoms, Causes, and Treatment of Diseases, and Directions in Dislocations and Fractures; with Advice on the Preservation of Health in Hot Climates* (Boston, 1834) 6, 9; Usher Parsons, *Physicians for Ships: Containing Medical Advice for Seaman and Other Persons at Sea, on Treatment of Diseases, and on the Preservation of Health in Sickly Climates, and Also on California* (Boston, 1851), 20; E.F. Plate and H.W. Bütter, *Directions for the Treatment of Diseases during a Voyage at Sea; with an Appendix Containing Useful Remarks and Observations* (Bremen, 1847), 12.

[24] Clapp, *Autobiographical Sketches*, 209; John Harrison, "Remarks on Yellow Fever," *Stethoscope* 5 (1855): 588-89; John C. Van Horne, ed., *The Correspondence and Miscellaneous Papers of Benjamin Henry Latrobe* (Baltimore, 1988), 3:311.

[25] Wight, *Seaman's Guide*, 7-9.

[26] Jerah Johnson, *Congo Square in New Orleans* (New Orleans, 1995), 2-4; James H. Cassedy, *Medicine and American Growth, 1800-1860* (Madison, WI, 1986), 119.

[27] Pritchett, "Strangers'Disease," 518-19, 529; Kenneth F. Kiple and Virginia H. Kiple, "Black Yellow Fever Immunities Innate and Acquired, as Revealed in the American South," *Social Science History* 1 (1977): 425-29; Todd L. Savitt, *Medicine and Slavery: The Diseases and Health Care of Blacks in Antebellum Virginia* (Urbana, IL, 1978), 240-46.

[28] Bloom, *Yellow Fever Epidemic of 1878*, 11; "Science and Health," *Scientific American*, new series, 29 (1873): 345.

[29] Savitt, *Medicine and Slavery*, 241; P.A.K. Addy, et al., "Possible Contributing Factors to the Paucity of Yellow Fever Epidemics in the Ashanti Region of Ghana, West Africa," *East African Medical Journal* 73 (1996): 3.

[30] Everett, "Epidemic of 1853," 395 (quotation, p. 394); Savitt, *Medicine and Slavery*, 240-46; [Thomas Hamilton], *Men and Manners in America* (Philadelphia, 1833), 310.

[31] Florence, *New Orleans Cemeteries*, 78.

[32] Carrigan, "Yellow Fever Scourge" 62; Duffy, *Sword of Pestilence*, 14.

[33] Goldfield, "The Business of Health Planning," 568; "Health of New Orleans," *De Bow's Commercial Review*, 1 (April 1846), 382.

[34] Niehaus, "The New Irish," 380-81; "Health of New Orleans," *De Bow's Commercial Review*, 382.

[35] Elliott Ashkenazi, *The Business of Jews in Louisiana, 1840-1875* (Tuscaloosa, AL, 1988), 126; Bertram Wallace Korn, *The Early Jews of New Orleans* (Waltham, MA, 1969), 172-73.

[36] Samuel Wilson, et al., eds., *Queen of the South, New Orleans, 1853-1862: The Journal of Thomas K. Wharton* (New Orleans and New York, 1999), 102; William W. Chenault and Robert C. Reinders, "The Northern-Born Community of New Orleans in the 1850s," 439.

[37] Joann P. Krieg, *A Whitman Chronology* (Iowa City, 1998), xix, 19-20; Edwin H. Miller, ed., *Selected Letters of Walt Whitman* (Iowa City, 1990), quotation, p. 19.

NOTES
TO CHAPTER THREE

[1] "Yellow Fever in New Orleans and Mortality of New York," *The Illustrated London News*, 263; Niehaus, "The New Irish," 378; Gardner, *New Orleans Directory, 1858*, 382.

[2] "Editor's Easy Chair," *Harper's New Monthly Magazine* 7 (1853): 846.

[3] W.C. Corsan, *Two Months In The Confederate States: An Englishmen's Travels Through the South*, ed. Benjamin H. Trask (Baton Rouge, 1996), 11-12; Patterson, "Yellow Fever Epidemics;" Duffy, *Sword of Pestilence*, 167; Carrigan, *Saffron Scourge*, 80; Reginald Horsman, *Josiah Nott of Mobile: Southerner, Physician, and Racial Theorist* (Baton Rouge, 1987), 139; Gardner, *New Orleans Directory, 1858*, 382.

[4] Emmeline Stuart Wortley, *Travels in the United States, etc. during 1849 and 1850*, 3 vols. (London, 1851), 1:226-28.

[5] Jane M.C. Turnbull and Marion Turnbull, *American Photographs*, 2 vols. (London, 1859), 2:43-44 (first quotation), 58 (second and third quotations); Wilson, *Journal of Thomas K. Wharton*, 104 (fourth quotation), 172 (fifth quotation).

[6] *The Epidemic Summer: List of Interments in All the Cemeteries of New Orleans from the First of May to the First of November, 1853* (New Orleans, 1853), xii; Duffy, *Sword of Pestilence*, 167; Carrigan, *Saffron Scourge*, 80.

[7] "New Orleans.—The Yellow Fever," *Illustrated London News* 23 (September 24, 1853): 244; "Yellow Fever in New Orleans and Mortality of New York," *Illustrated London News*, 263; Duffy, *Sword of Pestilence*, 69; *The Epidemic Summer*, xii; Robinson, *Diary of a Samaritan*, 150-52.

[8] Carrigan, "Privilege, Prejudice, and the Strangers' Disease," 571.

[9] John Freeman to Brother, October 16, 1855, John Young Freeman Papers, L.R. Wilson Library, Southern Historical Collection, University of North Carolina-Chapel Hill.

[10] Gleeson, *Irish in the South*, 46-48; Carrigan, "Privilege, Prejudice, and the Strangers' Disease," 572-75 (quotation, p. 575); R. Dudley Edwards and T. Desmond Williams, eds., *The Great Famine: Studies in Irish History 1845-52* (New York, 1957), 266-68.

[11] Plate, *Diseases during a Voyage at Sea*, 11-13.

[12] Wilson, *Journal of Thomas K. Wharton*, 47, 97, 176, 177, 180; Clapp, *Autobiographical Sketches*, 185-89, 210-11; Harold Sinclair, *The Port of New Orleans* (New York, 1942), 212-15; Robinson, *Diary of a Samaritan* (New York, 1860), 70, 150-52, 167, 186; Hall, *Manhattaner in New Orleans*, 68-71.

[13] Wilson, *Journal of Thomas K. Wharton*, 47, 97, 176, 177, 180; Clapp, *Autobiographical Sketches*, 185-89, 210-11; Sinclair, *Port of New Orleans*, 212-15; Benjamin H. Trask, "Yellow Fever and Its Effects on Southern American Ports, 1850 to 1905," *Mariners' Museum Journal*, 2d series, 2 (1996): 45-54; Hall, *Manhattaner in New Orleans*, 68-71; Florence, *New Orleans Cemeteries*, 32; Bennet Dowler, *Tableau of the Yellow Fever of 1853, Topographical, Chronological, and Historical Sketches, The Epidemics of New Orleans Since Their Origin in 1796 Illustrative of the Quarantine Question* (New Orleans, 1854), quotation, p. 62.

[14] Wilson, *Journal of Thomas K. Wharton*, 183 (first quotation), 184 (second quotation).

[15] Salvaggio, *Charity Hospital*, 69; Harrison, "Remarks on Yellow Fever," 588 (second quotation, p. 595).

[16] Harrison, "Remarks on Yellow Fever," 610-24 (quotation, p. 610).

[17] Jo Ann Carrigan, "Yellow Fever in New Orleans, 1853: Abstractions and Realities," *Journal of Southern History* 25 (1959): 350.

[18] Fenner, *Yellow Fever at New Orleans, 1853*, 18 (first and second quotation), 23 (last quotation); Griffith, *Universal Formulary*, remaining quotations, p. 293.

[19] Duffy, *Sword of Pestilence*, 104; *Report of the Joint Committee on Public Health: Majority Report* (New Orleans, 1854) 6n; Horne, *Correspondence of Benjamin H. Latrobe*, 3:1066.

[20] E.H. Barton, *The Cause and Prevention of Yellow Fever at New Orleans and Other Cities in America* (New York, 1857), viii-xv; Matas, "Yellow Fever Retrospect," 455; Cassedy, *Medicine and American Growth*, 42-43.

[21] Hall, *Manhattaner in New Orleans*, 69; Hildreth, *Howard Association*, 104; Gardner, *New Orleans Directory, 1858*, 331-32, 346-47.

[22] John Harley Warner, "The Idea of Southern Medical Distinctiveness: Medical Knowledge and Practice in the Old South," in Ronald L. Numbers and Todd L. Savitt, eds., *Science and Medicine in the Old South* (Baton Rouge, 1989), 199; *Report of the Select Committee of the Senate of the United States on the Sickness and Mortality on board Emigrant Ships* (New York, 1977), 145; *Report of the Joint Committee on Public Health: Majority Report* (New Orleans, 1854), 4; Gleeson, *The Irish in the South*, 19, 26-27; Salvaggio, *Charity Hospital*, 47.

[23] Fenner, *Yellow Fever at New Orleans, 1853*, 17-29, 71; Salvaggio, *Charity Hospital*, 49.

[24] "Editor's Easy Chair," *Harper's New Monthly Magazine*, 703 (quotation); Thomas P. Kettell, *Southern Wealth and Northern Profits; As Exhibited in Statisti-*

cal Facts and Offical [sic] *Figures: Showing the Necessity of Union to the Future Prosperity and Welfare of the Republic* (Tuscaloosa, AL, 1965), x, 106.

[25] *New York Herald* (September 6, 1853).

[26] Hobson Woodward, "'Through the Furnace of Affliction:' A Connecticut Family in the New Orleans Epidemic of 1853," *National Genealogical Society Quarterly* 89 (2001): 113-32.

[27] Carrigan, "Yellow Fever Abstractions and Realities," 340-41; Charles E. Rosenberg, *The Cholera Years: The United States in 1832, 1849, and 1866* (Chicago, 1987), 40-54.

[28] John P. Ordway, *Let Me Kiss Him for His Mother* (Boston, 1859).

[29] Barton, *Cause and Prevention of Yellow Fever*, viii-xv; Matas, "Yellow Fever Retrospect," 455.

[30] Gordon Earl Gillson, "The Louisiana State Board of Health: The Formative Years" (Ph.D. dissertation, Louisiana State University, 1960), 226.

[31] Everett, "Epidemic of 1853;" M. Morton Dowler, "On the Reputed Causes of Yellow Fever, and the So Called Sanitary Measures of the Day," *Stethoscope* 5 (1855): 638.

[32] Robinson, *Diary of a Samaritan*, 185; Howard Association, *Report of the Howard Association Epidemic of 1853* (New Orleans, 1853), 28 (quotation, p. 27).

[33] Korn, *Early Jews of News Orleans*, 231-32; Gardner, *New Orleans Directory, 1858*, 390; *The Story of the Jewish Orphans Home New Orleans* (New Orleans, 1906), passim.

[34] Fenner, *Yellow Fever at New Orleans, 1853*, 71; Salvaggio, *Charity Hospital*, 74-75.

[35] Duffy, *Sword of Pestilence*, 119-26; *Report of the Howard Association of Norfolk, Va.*, (Philadelphia, 1857), 49-53, 94 (first quotation, p. 51; second quotation, p. 53).

[36] *Howard Association of Norfolk, Va.*, 49-50; Erasmus D. Fenner to St. Julian Ravenel, September 21, 1855; Harriott, Horry, and Ravenel Family Paper, South Carolina Historical Society, Charleston, S.C.

[37] *Howard Association of Norfolk, Va.*, 61 (first quotation), 62 (second quotation); "Two Noble Women," *Harper's Weekly* 1 (June 6, 1857), 353.

[1] *Liberator* [Boston] (October 12, 1855); Robert H. Bremner, *The Public Good: Philanthropy and Welfare in the Civil War Era* (New York, 1980), 17.

[2] Warner, "Southern Medical Distinctiveness" in *Science and Medicine in the Old South*, 193-97; John Duffy, "Sectional Conflict and Medical Education in Louisiana," *Journal of Southern History* 23 (1957): 290.

[3] Charles Lee Lewis, *David Glasgow Farragut: Admiral in the Making* (Annapolis, 1941), 162-63; Loyall Farragut, *Life of David Glasgow Farragut* (New York, 1879), 8.

[4] Benjamin F. Butler, *Butler's Book: A Review of His Legal, Political, and Military Career* (Boston, 1892), 42

[5] Ibid., 403; *Official Report of the War of the Rebellion: A Compilation of the Records of the Union and Confederate Armies*, 70 vols. (hereafter cited as *O.R.*) (Washington, D.C., 1880-1901), Series I, Vol. 6, quotation p. 716.

[6] Butler, *Butler's Book*, 394 (first quotation), 404 (second quotation); *O.R.* Ser. I, Vol. 6, 724.

[7] Julia Ellen (LeGrand) Waltz, "The Journal of Julia LeGrand" in Katherine M. Jones, ed., *Heroines of Dixie: Spring of High Hopes* (St. Simons Island, GA, 1979), 136; Gillison, *Louisiana State Board of Health*, quotation, p. 177.

[8] Ashkenazi, *Diary of Clara Solomon*, 370 (quotation, p. 350).

[9] John D. Winters, *The Civil War in Louisiana*, (Baton Rouge, 1991), 130; Butler, *Butler's Book*, 404.

[10] Thomas Hewson Bache, *Some Practical Observations on Yellow Fever, Published for the Use of Surgeons of the Volunteer Forces in the Department of the Gulf* (New Orleans, 1862), 3 (first quotation), 11 (second quotation).

[11] Ibid., passim; *Daily Journal* [Wilmington, N.C.], (September 27, 1862).

[12] *Harper's Weekly* 7 (April 25, 1863), 270 (first and second quotations); Ibid. (May 30, 1863), 351 (third quotation); Ibid. (October 3, 1863), 640.; Ibid. (July 18, 1863), 463 (fourth quotation); George Washington Cable, *Strong Hearts* (New York, 1913), 131; Quitman Kohnke, "The Mosquito Question," *Scientific American Supplement* (February 4, 1905), 24328.

[13] *O.R.*, Ser. I, Vol. 7, 294.

[14] "Diary and Correspondence of Salmon P. Chase," *Annual Report of the American Historical Association for the Year 1902* (New York, 1971) 2:297-99 (quotation, p. 306).

[15] Ibid., 306-319 (first quotation, p. 309; second quotation, p. 311; and third quotation, p. 311).

[16] Winters, *Civil War in Louisiana*, 129.

[17] *The Medical and Surgical History of the Civil War*, 15 vols. (Wilmington, N.C., 1991), 4:676; Benjamin F. Butler to Captain of the Spanish War Steamer "Blaso De Garay," August 11, 1862; José Manuel Diaz de Herrera to Major General Benj. F. Butler (translation), August 13, 1862; quotation Benjamin F. Butler to Señor Don Calleja, August 16, 1862; Benjamin F. Butler to Sir (Commander of Spanish War Steamer) August 19, 1862, Benjamin F. Butler Papers, Manuscript Collections, Library of Congress.

[18] Juan Callejon to the Consul of H. C. Majesty, August 11, 1862 (translation), Butler Papers.

[19] Jo Ann Carrigan, "Yankees Versus Yellow Jack Fever in New Orleans, 1862-1866," *Civil War History* 9 (1963): 249; Gillison, *Louisiana State Board of Health*, 181.

[20] Corsan, *Two Months in the Confederate States*, 18.

[21] *O.R.*, Ser. I, Vol. 6, 889; Wilson, *Journal of Thomas K. Wharton*, 47, 175; Winters, *Civil War in Louisiana*, 122, 141.

[22] Charles East, ed., *Sarah Morgan: The Civil War Diary of a Southern Woman* (New York, 1992), 107.

[23] R.R. Barrow to D.F. Fenner, September 11, 1862, John Thomas Pickett Papers, Manuscript Collections, Library of Congress; Elizabeth A. Fenn, *Pox Americana: The Great Smallpox Epidemic of 1775-82* (New York, 2002), 88-89.

[24] Gillison, *Louisiana State Board of Health*, 182-83.

[25] *Medical and Surgical History*, 4:675; Elisha Harris, "The Public Health," *North American Review* 127 (November-December 1878): 444 (first quotation, p. 445); *Marine Journal* 11 (December 8, 1888): second quotation, p. 9.

[26] Joseph G. Dawson, III, *Army Generals and Reconstruction, 1862-1877* (Baton Rouge, 1982), 151-52; Hildreth, *Howard Association*, 116-17, 123; Kiple, "Black Yellow Fever Immunities," 427.

[27] Florence, *New Orleans Cemeteries*, 115-17.

[1] Dawson, *Army Generals and Reconstruction*, 151-61, 222; *Medical and Surgical History* 4, 683.

[2] Gillison, *Louisiana State Board of Health*,188-89; Gibson, *William C. Gorgas*, 76-94.

[3] Carrigan, *Saffron Scourge*, 274; John P. Dyer, *Tulane: The Biography of a University, 1834-1865* (New York, 1966), 71-72, 324, Hildreth, *Howard Association*, 140.

[4] Phyllis Allen Richmond, "American Attitudes Toward the Germ Theory of Disease (1860-1880)," *Journal of the History of Medicine and Allied Sciences* 9 (October 1954): 436-44.

[5] Edward King, *The Great South*, W. Magruder Drake and Robert R. Jones, eds. (Baton Rouge, 1972), 62.

[6] *Nautical Gazette* 7 (August 26, 1874): 134.

[7] "The Yellow Fever Alarm," *Nautical Gazette* 7 (September 16, 1874): 184; Ellis, *Yellow Fever & Public Health*, 74, 86-87.

[8] King, *The Great South*, 62.

[9] Michael A. Ross, "Justice Miller's Reconstruction: The Slaughter-House Cases, Health Codes, and Civil Rights in New Orleans," *Journal of Southern History* 54 (1988): 653-62; Gillison, *Louisiana State Board of Health*, 243-45.

[10] C. Spinzig, *Yellow Fever: Nature and Epidemic Character* (St. Louis, 1880), 181-200; James O. Breeden, "Joseph Jones and Public Health in the New South" *Louisiana History* 32 (1991): 361; John H. Ellis, "The New Orleans Yellow Fever Epidemic in 1878: A Note on the Affective History of Societies and Communities," *Clio Medica* 12 (1977): 194.

[11] C.B. White, *Disinfection in Yellow Fever as Practised* [sic] *in New Orleans in the Years 1870 to 1876 Inclusive* (New Orleans, 1876), 5-6, 13-15 (quotation, p. 6).

[12] Gillison, *Louisiana State Board of Health*, 237; "Science and Health," *Scientific American*, new series, 29 (November 29, 1873), 345; Hildreth, *Howard Association*, 124.

[13] "Yellow Fever in New Orleans in 1873," *Medical News and Library* 31 (December 1873): 190, quoting from the *New Orleans Medical and Surgical Journal* (November 1873); "Science and Health," *Scientific American*, 345; Gillison, *Louisiana State Board of Health*, 237.

[14] "Yellow Fever in New Orleans in 1873," *Medical News*, 190; "Science and Health," *Scientific American*, 345; Gillison, Louisiana State Board of Health, 237.

[15] Gillison, *Louisiana State Board of Health*, 200-28; Harris, "Public Health," 444-47.

[16] Ellis, *Yellow Fever & Public Health*, 71-72; Hildreth, *Howard Association*, 138.

[17] *A Compilation of the Messages and Papers of the Presidents*, 11 vols. (Washington, D.C., 1897), 6:4444; Bremner, *Public Good*, 195; "America," *Illustrated London News* 73 (September 14, 1878): 246.

[18] Nuwer, *Yellow Fever Epidemic of Mississippi*, 26-30.

[19] Hildreth, *Howard Association*, 131-32.

[20] Ellis, *Yellow Fever & Public Health*, 71; *Report of the Commissioner of Navigation to the Secretary of the Treasury, 1894* (Washington, D.C., 1894), 205; *Annual Report of the Commissioner of Navigation to the Secretary of Commerce and Labor* (Washington, D.C., 1906), 24.

[21] Hildreth, *Howard Association*, 133-36.

[22] Edwina Walls, "Observations on the New Orleans Yellow-Fever Epidemic, 1878," *Louisiana History* 23 (1982): 65.

[23] Ibid., 66.

[24] Ibid., 60-67 (quotation, p. 64).

[25] "Weekly Report of the Surgeon General of the Marine Hospital Service," *New York Maritime Register* 10 (August 31, 1878): n.p.; Nuwer, *Yellow Fever Epidemic of Mississippi*, 32, 43, 65.

[26] *Southern Historical Society Papers* 4 (October 1878): 192; Edward J. Blum, "The Crucible of Disease: Trauma, Memory, and National Reconciliation during the Yellow Fever Epidemic of 1878," *Journal of Southern History* 69 (November 2003): 804, 806; Société Française de Secours Mutuels de Lafayette of Brooklyn, subscription list number 13, September 8, 1878, Writer's Collection.

[27] Bremner, *Public Good*, 196; Hildreth, *Howard Association*, 134; "Gifts For The Fever-Stricken," *Harper's Weekly* 22 (October 29, 1878): 849 (quotation, p. 850); Bloom, *Yellow Fever Epidemic of 1878*, 204; Blum, "The Crucible of Disease," 797.

[28] Ellis, *Yellow Fever & Public Health*, 41, 59; Hildreth, *Howard Association*, 136, 146; Bloom, *Yellow Fever Epidemic of 1878*, 11; Ellis, "Yellow Fever Epidemic in 1878," 192-93.

[29] Caroline Elizabeth Merrick, *Old Times in Dixie Land: A Southern Matron's Memories* (New York, 1901), 116-20 (quotation, p. 119).

[30] George W. Cable to H.H. Boyensen, November 5, 1878, George Washington Cable Papers, Special Collection, Small Library, University of Virginia.

[31] Ibid.

[32] Ibid.

[33] Ibid.; Louis D. Rubin, Jr., *George W. Cable: The Life of and Times of a Southern Heretic* (New York, 1969), 72 (quotation, p. 73); George W. Cable, *Grandissimes: A Story of Creole Life* (New York, 1957), 11.

[34] Nuwer, *Yellow Fever Epidemic of Mississippi*, 76; Hildreth, *Howard Association*, 142-46.

[35] Hildreth, *Howard Association*, 142-46.

[36] *Report of the Relief Work of the Young Men's Christian Association of New Orleans in the Yellow Fever Epidemic of 1878* (New Orleans, 1879), 3, 7, 14, 40.

[37] Everett, "Epidemic of 1853," 404; Hildreth, *Howard Association*, 125.

[38] Margaret Humphreys, *Yellow Fever and the South* (New Brunswick, N.J., 1992), 87.

[39] "Disinfection by Cold," *Scientific American*, new series, 40 (February 22, 1879): 117; Patterson, "Yellow Fever Epidemics," 63; Ellis, *Yellow Fever & Public Health*, 59, 69-70; Nuwer, *Yellow Fever Epidemic of Mississippi*, 46-47; Bloom, *Yellow Fever Epidemic of 1878*, 212.

[40] Ellis, *Yellow Fever & Public Health*, 44, 149-50.

[41] Humphreys, *Yellow Fever and the South*, 89; "Cost of Yellow Fever," *Scientific American*, new series, 40 (January 11, 1879): 24 (quotation).

[42] "The Probable Starting Point of the Yellow Fever," *Scientific American*, new series, 39 (November 30, 1878): 340; William Ivy Hair, *Bourbonism and Agrarian Protest* (Baton Rouge, 1969), 73; "Yellow Fever in Winter," *Scientific American*, new series, 40 (March 22, 1879): 180.

[43] "Yellow Fever in New Orleans in 1873," *Medical News*, 190; Nuwer, *Yellow Fever Epidemic of Mississippi*, 26-29.

[44] Harry James Brown and Frederick D. Williams, eds., *The Diary of James A Garfield, 1878-1881*, 4 vols. (East Lansing, MI, 1981), 4:158 (first quotation), 176 (second quotation).

[45] "Dr. S.M. Bemiss," *Southern Bivouac* 3 (December 1884): 187-88; Breeden, "Joseph Jones," 361; Ellis, *Yellow Fever & Public Health*, 119; Bess Furman, *A Profile of the United States Public Health Service, 1798-1948* (Washington, D.C., [1949?]), 151; "American Public Health Association" *Scientific American*, new series, 41 (November 29, 1879): 226-27.

[46] *Marine Journal* 10 (July 28, 1888): 2; Williams, *United States Public Health Service*, 68-69, 79, 82; Brown, *Diary of James A. Garfield*, 4:179-81.

[47] Williams, *United States Public Health Service*, 82, 89.

[48] Breeden, "Joseph Jones," 361-62; Ellis, *Yellow Fever & Public Health*, 119; *Report of the Commissioner of Navigation to the Secretary of the Treasury, 1887* (Washington, D.C., 1888), 131.

[49] *American National Biography*, 12:223-24; Ellis, *Yellow Fever & Public Health*, 119; Breeden, "Joseph Jones," 363-65.

[50] John Gamgee, *Yellow Fever: A Nautical Disease, Its Origin and Prevention* (New York 1879): 147 (first quotation); "Disinfection by Cold," *Scientific American*, new series, 40 (February 22, 1879): 117 (second quotation); "Frost and Fever," *Scientific American*, new series, 40 (April 26, 1879): 256 (third quotation); Carrigan "Yellow Fever Scourge," 56.

[51] "Yellow Fever in Winter," *Scientific American*, 180; Gillison, *Louisiana State Board of Health*, 254-56.

[52] Richard M. McMurry, *John Bell Hood and the War for Southern Independence* (Lexington, KY, 1982), 193-203; "In Memory of General J. B. Hood," *Southern Historical Society Papers* 32 (1904): 156; Bloom, *Yellow Fever Epidemic of 1878*, 218-19.

[53] McMurry, *John Bell Hood*, 193-203.

[54] *New York Times* (March 3, 1879).

NOTES
TO CHAPTER SIX

[1] Gleeson, *Irish in the South,* 88, 90; Anne Commire, ed., *Women in World History: A Biographical Encyclopedia,* 17 vols. (Detroit, 2000), 7:68.

[2] Mrs. T.P. O'Connor, *My Beloved South* (New York, 1914), 205-06.

[3] *Women in World History,* 7:68; *Report of the Jacksonville Auxiliary Sanitary Association of Jacksonville, Florida: Covering the Work of the Association During the Yellow Fever Epidemic, 1888* (Jacksonville, FL, 1889), 141, 40 [appendix].

[4] Dyer, *Tulane University,* 71-72.

[5] Breeden, "Joseph Jones," 341-46, 366-69.

[6] Joseph Holt, *An Epitomized Review of the Principles and Practice of Maritime Sanitation* (New Orleans, 1892), 39-41, 56.

[7] Ibid., 79-80.

[8] Ibid., passim.

[9] Ibid., 7-9; Joy J. Jackson, "The Port of New Orleans in the Gilded Age," *Gulf Coast Historical Review* 10 (1994): 196-97.

[10] C.P. Wilkinson, "The Period of Incubation of Yellow Fever Among Passengers and Crews of Vessels from Infected Ports," *New Orleans Medical and Surgical Journal,* new series, 17 (1889): 397.

[11] Mark Aldrich, "Train Wrecks to Typhoid Fever: The Development of Railroad Medicine Organizations, 1850 to World War I," *Bulletin of the History of Medicine* 75 (2001): 279-80.

[12] Louisville & Nashville R.R. Co., "Yellow Fever Bulletin," Circular No. 2133 (November 19, 1897), Writer's Collection; *Shipping Gazette & Lloyd's List Weekly Summary* (October 8, 1897).

[13] "American Public Health Association," *Scientific American,* 226-27; G.B. Young, "Train-Inspection Service," in *Yellow Fever Studies* (New York, 1977), 121-43.

[14] Young, "Train-Inspection Service," 121-43 (quotation, p. 124).

[15] *Marine Journal* 9 (September 29, 1888), 10; Breeden, "Joseph Jones," 359; Holt, *Maritime Sanitation,* 5, 11 (quotation, p. 7).

[16] "National Quarantine," *Marine Journal* 11 (October 27, 1888): 9.

[17] Williams, *United States Public Health Service*, 84, 165-67; Wyndham D. Miles, "Prizes for Yellow Fever Research in the 1880's," *Bulletin for the History of Medicine* 43 (1969): 176-79; Howard Markel, *Quarantine!: East European Jewish Immigrants and the New York City Epidemics of 1892* (Baltimore, 1997), 137-52.

[18] James S. Zachaire, *New Orleans Guide (New Orleans*, 1893), 92 (first quotation), 93 (second quotation).

[19] Kohnke, "The Mosquito Question," 24346.

[20] Jackson, "New Orleans in the Gilded Age," 196-97; "New Orleans Chamber of Commerce," *Marine News* 11 (December 8, 1888): 9.

[21] William Watson, *Life in the Confederate Army: Being the Observations and Experiences of an Alien in the South During the American Civil War* (Baton Rouge, 1995), 20; *Marine Journal* 10 (September 8, 1888): 9.

[22] Walter Reed, et al., "The Etiology of Yellow Fever: A Preliminary Note," *Philadelphia Medical Journal* 6 (October 27, 1900): 790-96.

[23] C.P. Wilkinson to Henry B. Horlbeck, July 2, 1899, Dr. Henry Horlbeck Papers, South Carolina Historical Society, Charleston, S.C; Peggy Haile McPhillips and Benjamin H. Trask, "The Darker Side of Commerce: Yellow Fever and the Chesapeake Bay," *Chesapeake Bay Maritime Museum Quarterly* 1 (2003-2004): 17.

NOTES
TO CHAPTER SEVEN

[1] Reed, "Etiology of Yellow Fever," 790-96, William B. Bean, *Walter Reed: A Biography* (Charlottesville, VA, 1982), 142-43, 159-64.

[2] Marshall Scott Legan, "The War of the Waters: The Louisiana-Mississippi Quarantine War of 1905," *Journal of Mississippi History* 50 (1988): 89.

[3] Kohnke, "The Mosquito Question," 24328; Humphreys, *Yellow Fever and the South*, 151-52; Reginald B. Leech, "The Mosquito Theory, Yellow Fever and Arsenization," *North American Review* 187 (1908): 100-105.

[4] "Yellow Fever Prevented By Mosquito Extermination," *Scientific American* 93 (August 5, 1905): 99.

[5] Jo Ann Carrigan, "Mass Communication and Public Health: The 1905 Campaign Against Yellow Fever in New Orleans," *Louisiana History* 29 (1988): 5.

[6] Jean Ann Scarpaci, "Immigrants in the New South: Italians in Louisiana's Sugar Parishes, 1880-1910," in Milton Cantor, ed., *American Workingclass Culture: Explorations in American Labor and Social History* (Westport, CT, 1979), 378, 391-95; Roger Daniels, *Not Like Us: Immigrants and Minorities in America, 1890-1924* (Chicago, 1997), 68-70.

[7] White, *Disinfection in Yellow Fever*, 8.

[8] Daniels, *Not Like Us*, 68-70.

[9] Bloom, *Yellow Fever Epidemic of 1878*, 271; [John Ellis] to Sis, September 8, 1905, Touro Infirmary Archives, New Orleans; "Yellow Fever Prevented By Mosquito Extermination," *Scientific American*, 99; Carrigan, "Mass Communication and Public Health," 6; Pietro Di Donato, *Immigrant Saint: The Life of Mother Cabrini* (New York, 1990), [i-iii], 181-83.

[10] Bloom, *Yellow Fever Epidemic of 1878*, 271; "Yellow Fever Prevented By Mosquito Extermination," *Scientific American*, 99; Carrigan, "Mass Communication and Public Health," 6; Williams, *United States Public Health Service*, 118; Jo Ann Carrigan, "Yellow Fever in New Orleans, 1905: The Last Epidemic," *Bulletin of the Tulane University Medical Faculty* 26 (1967): 20.

[11] Williams, *United States Public Health Service*, 118; Carrigan, "The Last Epidemic," 24; [John Ellis] to Sis, September 8, 1905, Touro Infirmary Archives.

[12] John R. Kemp, ed., *Martin Behrman of New Orleans: Memoirs of a City Boss* (Baton Rouge, 1977), 132; Williams, *United States Public Health Service*, 118; Carrigan, "The Last Epidemic," 24.

[13] Williams, *United States Public Health Service*, 118; Legan, "Quarantine War of 1905," *Journal of Mississippi History* 50 (1988): 92; Kohnke "The Mosquito Question," 24345.

[14] Carrigan, "The Last Epidemic," 22-23.

[15] "Yellow Fever Prevented By Mosquito Extermination," *Scientific American*, 99; [John Ellis] to Sis, September 8, 1905, Touro Infirmary Archives; Kohnke, "The Mosquito Question," 24346.

[16] Holt, *Maritime Sanitation*, 31-33 (quotation, p. 32).

[17] Williams, *United States Public Health Service*, 118; Legan, "Quarantine War of 1905," 91, 93; *Shipping Gazette & Lloyd's List Weekly Summary* (August 4, 1905).

[18] Carrigan, "The Last Epidemic," 24-25; "Certificate of Health," Wisner, LA, August 13, 1905, Writer's Collection.

[19] Kohnke, "The Mosquito Question," 24346.

[20] *Shipping Gazette & Lloyd's List Weekly Summary* (August 4, 1905); Kohnke, "The Mosquito Question," 24346.

[21] J.W. Bostick to N.C. Blanchard, August 1, 1905; N.C. Blanchard to Sec. Shaw, [telegram] August 3, 1905; J.H. Quinan to Sec. Shaw, September 23, 1905, Records of the U.S. Coast Guard, U.S. Revenue Cutter Service Vessels Correspondence Related to the Yellow Fever Patrol, 1905, Record Group 26, National Archives and Record Administration, Washington, D.C.

[22] Secretary of the Treasure Bay Oyster Company to S.P. Edmonds, USCG Records, Yellow Fever Patrol, 1905, NARA.

[23] John S. Callaghan to James R. Garfield, August 4, 1905 and attached newspaper clipping titled "The Winona Controversy;" S.R. Edmonds to Sec. Shaw, October 28, 1905, USCG Records, Yellow Fever Patrol, 1905, NARA.

[24] J.H. Quinan to W.G. Ross, September 4, 1905; Worth G. Ross to Sec. of Treas., August 26, 1905, USCG Records, Yellow Fever Patrol, 1905, NARA.

[25] Kemp, *Martin Behrman*, quotations, p. 145.

[26] Ibid., 141.

[27] Ibid., 140; "The Need For Federal Quarantine Control," *Scientific American* 93 (October 14, 1905): 294.

[28] Leech, "Arsenization," 100-05 (quotation, p. 104); Estes, *Dictionary of Protopharmacology*, 19; Kemp, *Martin Behrman*, 145-46.

[29] *New York Evening Post,* October 27, 1905 (photocopy), M.A. Styles Collection, Theodore Roosevelt Collection, Houghton Library, Harvard University, Cambridge, MA.

[30] Kemp, *Martin Behrman,* 150.

[31] Williams, *The United States Public Health Service,* 118; Legan, "Quarantine War of 1905," 90; [John Ellis] to Sis, September 8, 1905, Touro Infirmary Archives, New Orleans, LA.

[32] Carrigan "Yellow Fever Scourge," 56.

NOTES
TO EPILOGUE

[1] Patterson, "Yellow Fever," 864.

[2] Grace King, *New Orleans: The Place and the People* (New York, 1915), 280.

[3] Susan E. Robertson, et al., "Yellow Fever: A Decade of Reemergence," *Journal of the American Medical Association* 276 (1996): 1157.

[4] Frederick A. Murphy, "New, Emerging, and Reemerging Infectious Diseases," in Karl Maramorosch, et al., eds., *Advances in Virus Research* 43 (San Diego, 1994): 16; Robertson, "Yellow Fever: A Decade of Reemergence," 1157.

[5] Michael D'Antonio, "Making a New Mosquito," *Discover* 22 (May 2001): 66.

[6] Joy M. McFarland, et al., "Imported Yellow Fever in a United States Citizen," *Clinical Infectious Diseases* 25 (1997): 1143-46 (quotation, p. 1144).

[7] *USA Today* (August 7, 2002).

[8] "SARS Coverup Spurs A Shakeup on Beijing," *Washington Post* (April 21, 2003).

SELECTED BIBLIOGRAPHY

<u>Books</u>

Barton, E.H. *The Cause and Prevention of Yellow Fever at New Orleans and Other Cities in America*. 3d ed. New York: H. Bailliere, 1857.

Bloom, Khaled J. *The Mississippi Valley's Great Yellow Fever Epidemic of 1878*. Baton Rouge: Louisiana State University Press, 1993.

Brasseaux, Carl A., ed. *A Refuge For All Ages: Immigration in Louisiana History*. Volume 10, Louisiana Purchase Bicentennial Series in Louisiana History. Lafayette, LA: Center For Louisiana Studies, 1996.

Bremner, Robert H. *The Public Good: Philanthropy and Welfare in the Civil War Era*. New York: Alfred A. Knopf, 1980.

Butler, Benjamin F. *Butler's Book: A Review of His Legal, Political, and Military Career*. Boston: A.M. Thayer & Co., 1892.

Carrigan, Jo Ann. *The Saffron Scourge: A History of Yellow Fever in Louisiana, 1796-1905*. Lafayette, LA: Center for Louisiana Studies, 1994.

Carter, Edward C., II, et al., eds. *The Journals of Benjamin Henry Latrobe 1799-1820: From Philadelphia to New Orleans*. 3 vols. Baltimore and New Haven: Maryland Historical Society and Yale University Press, 1980.

Clapp, Theodore. *Autobiographical Sketches and Recollections during a Thirty-five Years' Residence in New Orleans*. Boston: Phillips, Sampson & Co., 1857.

Corsan, William C. *Two Months in the Confederate States: An Englishman's Travels Through the South*, edited by Benjamin H. Trask. Baton Rouge: Louisiana State University Press, 1996.

Cumings, Samuel. *The Western Pilot; Containing Charts of the Ohio River, and of the Mississippi*. Cincinnati: N. & G. Guilford & Co., 1834.

Dawson, Joseph G., III. *Army Generals and Reconstruction, 1862-1877*. Baton Rouge: Louisiana State University Press, 1982.

Selected Bibliography

Dowler, Bennet. *Tableau of the Yellow Fever of 1853, Topographical, Chronological, and Historical Sketches, The Epidemics of New Orleans Since Their Origin in 1796 Illustrative of the Quarantine Question.* New Orleans: Picayune, 1854.

Duffy, John. *Sword of Pestilence: The New Orleans Yellow Fever Epidemic of 1853.* Baton Rouge: Louisiana State University Press, 1966.

Dyer, John P. *Tulane: The Biography of a University, 1834-1865.* New York: Harper & Row, 1966.

Ellis, John H. *Yellow Fever & Public Health in the New South.* Lexington: University Press of Kentucky, 1992.

The Epidemic Summer: List of Interments in all the Cemeteries of New Orleans from the First of May to the First of November, 1853. New Orleans: True Delta, 1853.

Estes, J. Worth. *Dictionary of Protopharmacology: Therapeutic Practices, 1700-1850.* Canton, MA: Science History Publications, 1990.

Fenner, Erasmus Darwin. *History of the Epidemic Yellow Fever at New Orleans, Louisiana in 1853.* New York: Hall, Clayton & Co., 1854.

Florence, Robert. *New Orleans Cemeteries: Life in the Cities of the Dead.* New Orleans: Batture Press, 1997.

Gardner, Charles, comp. *Gardner & Wharton's New Orleans Directory, for the Year 1858.* New Orleans: E. C. Wharton, 1857.

Gibson, John M. *Physician To The World: The Life of General William C. Gorgas.* Durham, N.C.: Duke University Press, 1950.

Gleeson, David T. *The Irish in the South, 1815-1877.* Chapel Hill: University of North Carolina Press, 2001.

Hall, A. Oakley. *The Manhattaner in New Orleans: or Phases of "Crescent City" Life.* Edited by Henry Kmen. Baton Rouge: Louisiana State University Press, 1976.

Holt, Joseph. *An Epitomized Review of the Principles and Practice of Maritime Sanitation.* New Orleans: L. Graham & Son, 1892.

Howard Association. *Report of the Howard Association Epidemic of 1853.* New Orleans: Howard Association, 1853.

Humphreys, Margaret. *Yellow Fever and the South.* New Brunswick, NJ: Rutgers University Press, 1992.

Kemp, John R., ed. *Martin Behrman of New Orleans: Memoirs of a City Boss.* Baton Rouge: Louisiana State University Press, 1977.

Korn, Bertram Wallace. *The Early Jews of News Orleans.* Waltham, MA: American Jewish Historical Society, 1969.

Langley, Harold D. *A History of Medicine in the Early U.S. Navy.* Baltimore: Johns Hopkins University Press, 1995.

Markel, Howard. *Quarantine!: East European Jewish Immigrants and the New York City Epidemics of 1892.* Baltimore: Johns Hopkins University Press, 1997.

Merrick, Caroline E. *Old Times in Dixie Land: A Southern Matron's Memories.* New York: Grafton Press, 1901.

Moss, Kay K. *Southern Folk Medicine, 1750-1820.* Columbia: University of South Carolina Press, 1999.

Pitot, James. *Observations on the Colony of Louisiana from 1796 to 1802.* Baton Rouge: Louisiana State University Press, 1979.

Plate, E.F. and H.W. Bütter. *Directions for the Treatment of Diseases during a Voyage at Sea; with an Appendix Containing Useful Remarks and Observations.* Bremen: F.C. Dubers, 1847.

Report of the Joint Committee on Public Health: Majority Report. New Orleans: Emile La Sere, 1854.

Report of the Relief Work of the Young Men's Christian Association of New Orleans in the Yellow Fever Epidemic of 1878. New Orleans: A.H. Nelson, 1879.

Report of the Sanitary Commission of New Orleans on the Yellow Fever Epidemic of 1853; Published by Authority of the City Council of New Orleans. New Orleans: Picayune, 1854.

Robinson, William L. *The Diary of a Samaritan.* New York: Harper & Brothers, 1860.

Rowland, Dunbar, ed. *Official Letter Books of W.C.C. Claiborne, 1801-1816.* 6 vols. Jackson, MS: State Department of Archives and History, 1917.

Selected Bibliography

Salvaggio, John. *New Orleans' Charity Hospital: A Story of Physicians, Politics, and Poverty*. Baton Rouge: Louisiana State University Press, 1992.

Savitt, Todd L. *Medicine and Slavery: The Diseases and Health Care of Blacks in Antebellum Virginia*. Urbana: University of Illinois Press, 1978.

Savitt, Todd L. and James Harvey Young, eds. *Disease and Distinctiveness in the American South*. Knoxville: University of Tennessee Press, 1988.

Savitt, Todd L. and Ronald L. Numbers, eds. *Science and Medicine in the Old South*. Baton Rouge: Louisiana State University Press, 1989.

Spinzig, C. *Yellow Fever: Nature and Epidemic Character*. St. Louis: Geo. O. Rombold & Co., 1880.

Straus, Robert. *Medical Care For Seamen: The Origin of the Public Medical Service in the United States*. New Haven, CT and London: Yale University Press and Oxford University Press, 1950.

Van Horne, John C., ed. *The Correspondence and Miscellaneous Papers of Benjamin Henry Latrobe*. 3 vols. Baltimore and New Haven: Maryland Historical Society and Yale University Press, 1988.

Williams, Ralph Chester. *The United States Public Health Service, 1798-1950*. Washington, DC: Commissioned Officers Association of the United States Public Health Service, 1951.

Wilson, Samuel, ed. *Southern Travels: Journal of John H.B. Latrobe*. New Orleans: The Historic New Orleans Collection, 1986.

Wilson, Samuel, et al., eds. *Queen of the South, New Orleans, 1853-1862: The Journal of Thomas K. Wharton*. New Orleans and New York: The Historic New Orleans Collection and New York Public Library, 1999.

Winters, John D. *The Civil War in Louisiana*. Baton Rouge: Louisiana State University Press, 1991.

White, C.B. *Disinfection in Yellow Fever as Practised at New Orleans in the Years 1870 to 1876 Inclusive*. New Orleans: John W. Madden, 1876.

Yellow Fever Studies. New York: Arno Press, 1977.

Zacharie, James S. *New Orleans Guide*. New Orleans: F.F. Hansell & Bro., 1893.

Articles

Aldrich, Mark. "Train Wrecks to Typhoid Fever: The Development of Railroad Medicine Organizations, 1850 to World War I." *Bulletin of the History of Medicine* 75 (2001): 254-89.

Blake, John B. "Yellow Fever in the Continental United States During the Nineteenth Century America." *Bulletin of the New York Academy of Medicine* 44 (1968): 687-701.

Blum, Edward J. "The Crucible of Disease: Trauma, Memory, and National Reconciliation during the Yellow Fever Epidemic of 1878." *Journal of Southern History* 69 (2003): 791-820.

Breeden, James O. "Joseph Jones and Public Health in the New South." *Louisiana History* 32 (1991): 341-70.

Carrigan, Jo Ann. "Mass Communication and Public Health: The 1905 Campaign Against Yellow Fever in New Orleans." *Louisiana History* 29 (1988): 5-19.

————. "Privilege, Prejudice, and the Strangers' Disease in Nineteenth-Century New Orleans." *Journal of Southern History* 36 (1970): 568-78.

————. "Yankees Versus Yellow Jack Fever in New Orleans, 1862-1866." *Civil War History* 9 (1963): 248-60.

————. "Yellow Fever in New Orleans, 1853: Abstractions and Realities." *Journal of Southern History* 25 (1959): 339-55.

————. "Yellow Fever in New Orleans, 1905: The Last Epidemic." *Bulletin of the Tulane University Medical Faculty* 26 (1967): 19-28.

Doty, Alvah H. "The Scientific Prevention of Yellow Fever." *North American Review* 167 (1898): 681-89.

Dowler, M. Morton. "On the Reputed Causes of Yellow Fever, and the So Called Sanitary Measures of the Day." *Stethoscope* 4 (1855): 638-52.

Duffy, John. "Yellow Fever in the Continental United States During the Nineteenth Century." *Bulletin of the New York Academy of Medicine* 44 (1968): 687-701.

————. "Sectional Conflict and Medical Education in Louisiana." *Journal of Southern History* 23 (1957): 289-306.

Ellis, John H. "The New Orleans Yellow Fever Epidemic in 1878: A Note on the Affective History of Societies and Communities." *Clio Medica* 12 (1977): 189-216.

Everett, Donald E. "The New Orleans Yellow Fever Epidemic of 1853." *Louisiana Historical Quarterly* 33 (1950): 380-405.

Goldfield, David R. "The Business of Health Planning: Disease Prevention in the Old South." *Journal of Southern History* 42 (1976): 557-70.

Goodyear, James D. "The Sugar Connection: A New Perspective on the History of Yellow Fever." *Bulletin of the History of Medicine* 52 (1978): 5-21.

Harris, Elisha. "The Public Health." *North American Review* 127 (1878): 444-55.

Harrison, John. "Remarks on Yellow Fever." *Stethoscope* 5 (1855): 588-624.

"History and Incidents of the Plague in New Orleans." *Harper's New Monthly Magazine* 7 (1853): 797-806.

Holmes, Jack D.L. "The New Orleans Yellow Fever Epidemic of 1796 as seen by Baron de Pontalba." *Alabama Journal of Medical Sciences* 2 (1965): 205-15.

Kiple, K.F., and V.H. Kiple. "Black Yellow Fever Immunities Innate and Acquired, as Revealed in the American South." *Social Science History* 1 (1977): 419-36.

Leech, Reginald B. "The Mosquito Theory, Yellow Fever and Arsenization." *North American Review* 187 (1908): 100-105.

Legan, Marshall Scott. "The War of the Waters: The Louisiana-Mississippi Quarantine War of 1905." *Journal of Mississippi History* 50 (1988): 89-110.

Matas, Rudolph. "A Yellow Fever Retrospect and Prospect." *Louisiana Historical Quarterly* 8 (1925): 454-73.

Patterson, K. David. "Yellow Fever Epidemics and Mortality in the U.S., 1693-1905." *Social Science & Medicine* 34 (1992): 855-65.

Selected Bibliography

Porteous, Laura L., trans. "Sanitary Conditions in New Orleans Under the Spanish Regime, 1799-1800." *Louisiana Historical Quarterly* 15 (1932): 610-17.

Prichard, Walter, ed. "Three Letters of Richard Claiborne to William Miller, 1816-1818." *Louisiana Historical Quarterly* 24 (1941): 729-43.

Pritchett, Jonathan B. and İnsan Tunali. "Strangers' Disease: Determinants of Yellow Fever Mortality during the New Orleans Epidemic of 1853." *Explorations in Economic History* 32 (1995): 517-39.

Reed, Walter, et al. "The Etiology of Yellow Fever: A Preliminary Note." *Philadelphia Medical Journal* 6 (October 27, 1900): 789-96.

Robertson, Susan E., et al. "Yellow Fever: A Decade of Reemergence." *Journal of the American Medical Association* 276 (1996): 1157-62.

Trask, Benjamin H. "Yellow Fever and Its Effects on Southern American Ports, 1850 to 1905." *Mariners' Museum Journal,* 2nd Series, 2 (1996): 44-57.

"Yellow Fever of New Orleans in 1855." *Stethoscope* 5 (1855): 748-50.

Walls, Edwina. "Observations on the New Orleans Yellow-Fever Epidemic, 1878." *Louisiana History* 23 (1982): 60-67.

Woodward, Hobson. "'Through the Furnace of Affliction:' A Connecticut Family and New Orleans Yellow Fever Epidemic of 1853." *National Genealogical Society Quarterly* 89 (2001): 113-32.

Wilkinson, C.P. "The Period of Incubation of Yellow Fever Among Passengers and Crews of Vessels from Infected Ports." *New Orleans Medical and Surgical Journal* 17 [New Series] (December 1889): 393-98.

Dissertations

Gillson, Gordon Earl. "The Louisiana State Board of Health: The Formative Years." Ph.D. dissertation, Louisiana State University, 1960.

Hildreth, Flora Bassett. "The Howard Association of New Orleans, 1837-1878." Ph.D. dissertation, University of California-Los Angeles, 1978.

Nuwer, Deanne Love Stephens. "The 1878 Yellow Fever Epidemic of Mississippi." Ph.D. dissertation, University of Southern Mississippi, 1996.

Redard, Thomas E. "The Port of New Orleans: An Economic History, 1821-1850." 2 vols. Ph.D. dissertation, Louisiana State University and Agricultural and Mechanical College, 1985.

Newspapers and Weeklies

The Illustrated London News
Marine Journal
New Orleans Bee
New York Herald
New York Times
New York Maritime Register
Shipping Gazette & Lloyd's List Weekly Summary (London)
Scientific American

Manuscript Collections

Touro Infirmary Archives, New Orleans, LA:
Letter from Brother [John Ellis] to Sister, Sept. 8, 1905.

South Carolina Historical Society, Charleston, SC:
Dr. Henry Horlbeck Papers, 1888-1900.
Harriott, Horry, Ravenel Family Correspondence.

Southern Historical Collection, University of North Carolina at Chapel Hill:
John Freeman Young Papers.

Library of Congress, Washington, DC:
Benjamin Franklin Butler Papers.
John Thomas Pickett Papers.

Selected Bibliography

University of Virginia, Charlottesville, VA:
>   George Washington Cable Papers.
>   Randall Family Papers.

Harvard University, Cambridge, MA:
>   Theodore Roosevelt Collection.

National Archives and Record Administration, Washington, DC:
>   Record Group 26, Records of the US Coast Guard. U.S. Revenue Cutter Service Vessels Correspondence Related to the Yellow Fever Patrol, 1905.

Writer's Collection (Benjamin H. Trask), York County, VA.

IMAGE CREDITS

Cover, mosquito image from *A Handbook of the Mosquitoes of the Southeastern United States* by W.V. King, G.H. Bradley, Carroll N. Smith, and W.C. McDuffie (Washington D.C.: United States Department of Agriculture, 1960) transposed over *The City of New Orleans, and the Mississippi River. Lake Pontchartrain in the Distance* (New York: Currier & Ives, 1885); viii, *Harper's Weekly* (October 19, 1878), courtesy of the Mariners' Museum Library and Archives, Newport News, VA; 4, *Frank Leslie's Illustrated Newspaper* (September 28, 1878); 10 (left and right), photo collection of the Center for Louisiana Studies, University of Louisiana at Lafayette, Lafayette, LA; 11, enlarged from *Plan of the City and Suburbs of New Orleans from an Actual Survey made in 1815* by Jacques Tanesse (New Orleans, 1817); 14, from an 1850s print, courtesy the Historic New Orleans Collection, New Orleans, LA; 17, from *City of the Dead: A Journey Through St. Louis Cemetery #1, New Orleans, Louisiana* by Robert Florence (Lafayette: Center for Louisiana Studies, 1996); 20, photo collection of the Center for Louisiana Studies; 22, photo collection of the Center for Louisiana Studies; 25, *Frank Leslie's Illustrated Newspaper* (September 28, 1878); 29, from *Doctor Dispachemquic: A Story of the Great Southern Plague of 1878* by James Dugan (New Orleans: Clark and Hofeline, 1879), courtesy of the Louisiana and Lower Mississippi Valley Collection, Louisiana State University, Baton Rouge, LA; 36, title page of *History of the Yellow Fever in New Orleans during the Summer of 1853* (New Orleans: C.W. Kenworthy, 1854), courtesy of the Louisiana and Lower Mississippi Valley Collection; 39, from *To Glorious Immortality: The Rise and Fall of the Girod Street Cemetery* by Leonard Huber and Guy Bernard, (New Orleans: Alblen Books, 1961); 40-44, from *History of the Yellow Fever in New Orleans during the Summer of 1853*, courtesy of the Louisiana and Lower Mississippi Valley Collection; 48-49, from *The Cause and Prevention of Yellow Fever* by Edward H. Barton (Philadelphia: Lindsay and Blakiston, 1855), courtesy of the Louisiana and Lower Mississippi Valley Collection; 52, collection of Benjamin Trask; 55, courtesy of the Touro Infirmary Archives, New Orleans, LA; 57 (top), from New York *Daily Graphic* (September 11, 1878), courtesy of the Mariners' Museum Library and Archives; 57 (bottom), from *To Glorious Immortality* (1961); 60, from *The Life of Benjamin F. Butler* by T. A. Bland (Boston: Lee and Shepard Publishers, 1879); 63-64, from *Harper's Weekly* (April 25, May 30, July 18, and October 3, 1863); 70, collection of Benjamin Trask; 75, courtesy of the Mariners' Museum Library and Archives; 77, collection of Benjamin Trask; 80, courtesy of the Mariners' Museum Library and Archives; 81, from *Doctor Dispachemquic* by James Dugan (New Orleans, 1879), courtesy of the Louisiana and Lower Mississippi Valley Collection; 83, *Harper's New Monthly Magazine*, (May 1887); 86, New York *Daily Graphic* (September 11, 1878), collection of Benjamin Trask; 91, circa 1885 photograph by George François Mugnier, coursey the Louisiana State Museum, New Orleans, LA; 92, from *Battles and Leaders of the Civil War* by Robert Underwood Johnson and Clarence Clough Buel (New York: The Century Company, 1888); 93, from *The Gallant*

Index

Index